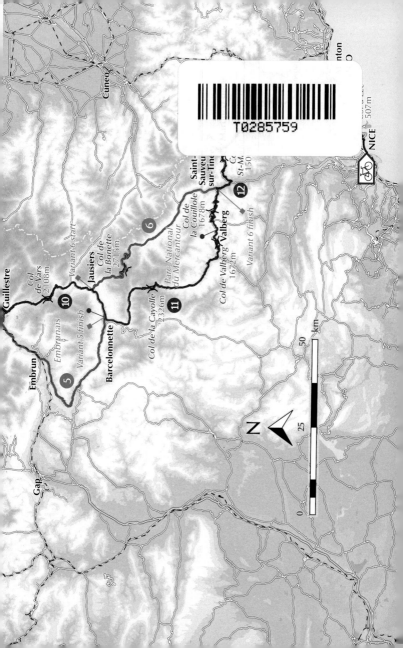

CYCLING THE ROUTE DES GRANDES ALPES

CYCLING THROUGH THE FRENCH ALPS FROM LAC LEMAN TO MENTON/NICE

by Giles Belbin

JUNIPER HOUSE, MURLEY MOSS,
OXENHOLME ROAD, KENDAL, CUMBRIA LA9 7RL
www.cicerone.co.uk

© Giles Belbin 2022
First edition 2022
ISBN: 978 1 78631 054 5

Printed in China on responsibly sourced paper on behalf of Latitude Press Ltd.
A catalogue record for this book is available from the British Library.
All photos are by Giles Belbin or James Chant, unless otherwise stated.

Route mapping by Lovell Johns www.lovelljohns.com
Contains OpenStreetMap.org data © OpenStreetMap
contributors, CC-BY-SA. NASA relief data courtesy of ESRI

Updates to this guide

While every effort is made by our authors to ensure the accuracy of guidebooks as they go to print, changes can occur during the lifetime of an edition. This guidebook was researched and written before the COVID-19 pandemic. While we are not aware of any significant changes to routes or facilities at the time of printing, it is likely that the current situation will give rise to more changes than would usually be expected. Any updates that we know of for this guide will be on the Cicerone website (www.cicerone.co.uk/1054/updates), so please check before planning your trip. We also advise that you check information about such things as transport, accommodation and shops locally. Even rights of way can be altered over time.

We are always grateful for information about any discrepancies between a guidebook and the facts on the ground, sent by email to updates@cicerone.co.uk or by post to Cicerone, Juniper House, Murley Moss, Oxenholme Road, Kendal, LA9 7RL.

Register your book: To sign up to receive free updates, special offers and GPX files where available, register your book at www.cicerone.co.uk.

Front cover: Riding to the Col de l'Iseran just outside Val d'Isère (Stage 6)

CONTENTS

Note on mapping

The route maps in this guide are derived from publicly available data, databases and crowd-sourced data. As such they have not been through the detailed checking procedures that would generally be applied to a published map from an official mapping agency. However, we have reviewed them closely in the light of local knowledge as part of the preparation of this guide.

The long road of the Galibier before the hairpin at Plan Lachat (Stage 8)

ROUTE SUMMARY TABLE

Stage	Start	Finish	Distance	Total ascent	Total descent	Page
1	Thonon-les-Bains	Cluses	58km (36 miles)	1070m	1013m	43
2	Cluses	La Clusaz	37km (23 miles)	1325m	742m	52
3	La Clusaz	Beaufort	51.75km (32 miles)	1350m	1683m	58
4	Beaufort	Bourg-Saint-Maurice	39.5km (24½ miles)	1495m	1418m	64
5	Bourg-Saint-Maurice	Val d'Isère	31.25km (19½ miles)	1285m	263m	70
6	Val d'Isère	Val Cenis Termignon	54.5km (34 miles)	1125m	1663m	76
7	Val Cenis Termignon	Valloire	51.5km (32 miles)	940m	833m	83
8	Valloire	Briançon	52.75km (32¾ miles)	1235m	1382m	90
9	Briançon	Guillestre	52.25km (32½ miles)	1575m	1795m	98
10	Guillestre	Barcelonnette	49.25km (30½ miles)	1170m	1069m	105
11	Barcelonnette	Valberg	75.25km (46¾ miles)	2400m	1862m	112
12	Valberg	Saint-Martin-Vésubie	58.75km (36½ miles)	1585m	2293m	120
13	Saint-Martin-Vésubie	Sospel	52km (32¼ miles)	1570m	2187m	127
14	Sospel	Nice	56km (34¾ miles)	1000m	1345m	134
		TOTAL	719.75km	19,125m	19,548m	

Variants

	Avoids	Adds	Start	Finish	Distance	Total ascent	Total descent	Page
1	Col d'Aravis and Col des Saisies (Stage 3)		Saint-Jean-de-Sixt	Villard-Sur-Doron	127km (79 miles)	1535m	1786m	142
2	Col de l'Iseran (Stage 5)	Col de la Madeleine	Bourg-Saint-Maurice	Saint-Michel-de-Maurienne	105.25km (65½ miles)	2330m	2428m	148
3	Col du Galibier (Stage 8)	Col du Mont Cenis	Val Cenis Lanslevillard	Briançon	95.5km (59½ miles)	2355m	2560m	155
4	Col du Galibier (Stage 8)	Col de la Croix de Fer	Saint-Michel-de-Maurienne	Col du Lautaret	119km (74 miles)	3700m	2359m	161
5	Col de Vars (Stage 10)		Guillestre	Barcelonnette	74.5km (46¼ miles)	860m	774m	169
6	Col de la Cayolle and Col de Valberg (Stage 11)	Col de la Bonette	Jausiers	Saint-Sauveur-sur-Tinée	74.75km (46½ miles)	1550m	2245m	175

Ride planner from Thonon-les-Bains

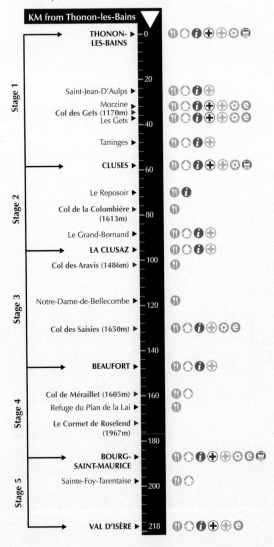

KM from Thonon-les-Bains

Stage 1

THONON-LES-BAINS ▶ — 0

— 20

Saint-Jean-D'Aulps ▶

Morzine ▶
Col des Gets (1170m) ▶
Les Gets ▶ — 40

Taninges ▶

CLUSES ▶ — 60

Stage 2

Le Reposoir ▶

Col de la Colombiére ▶ — 80
(1613m)

Le Grand-Bornand ▶

LA CLUSAZ ▶ — 100

Col des Aravis (1486m) ▶

Stage 3

Notre-Dame-de-Bellecombe ▶ — 120

Col des Saisies (1650m) ▶

— 140

BEAUFORT ▶

Col de Méraillet (1605m) ▶ — 160
Refuge du Plan de la Lai ▶

Le Cormet de Roselend ▶
(1967m) — 180

Stage 4

BOURG-SAINT-MAURICE ▶

Sainte-Foy-Tarentaise ▶ — 200

Stage 5

VAL D'ISÈRE ▶ — 218

Refreshments ⃝ **Accommodation** ⊕ **Hospital/Medical clinic** ⊕ **Pharmacy**
ⓘ **Tourist information** ✪ **Cycle shop** ⓔ **eBike charging** 🚆 **Rail station**

Ride planner from Thonon-les-Bains

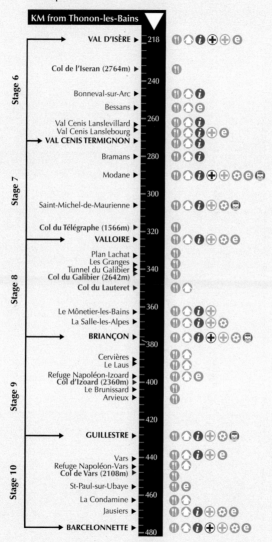

KM from Thonon-les-Bains

Stage	Location	KM
Stage 6	**VAL D'ISÈRE ▶**	218
	Col de l'Iseran (2764m) ▶	
		240
	Bonneval-sur-Arc ▶	
	Bessans ▶	
		260
	Val Cenis Lanslevillard ▶	
	Val Cenis Lanslebourg ▶	
	VAL CENIS TERMIGNON ▶	
Stage 7	Bramans ▶	280
	Modane ▶	
		300
	Saint-Michel-de-Maurienne ▶	
	Col du Télégraphe (1566m) ▶	320
	VALLOIRE ▶	
Stage 8	Plan Lachat ▶	
	Les Granges ▶	340
	Tunnel du Galibier ▶	
	Col du Galibier (2642m) ▶	
	Col du Lauteret ▶	
		360
	Le Mônetier-les-Bains ▶	
	La Salle-les-Alpes ▶	
	BRIANÇON ▶	
Stage 9		380
	Cervières ▶	
	Le Laus ▶	
	Refuge Napoléon-Izoard ▶	400
	Col d'Izoard (2360m) ▶	
	Le Brunissard ▶	
	Arvieux ▶	
		420
	GUILLESTRE ▶	
Stage 10		440
	Vars ▶	
	Refuge Napoléon-Vars ▶	
	Col de Vars (2108m) ▶	
	St-Paul-sur-Ubaye ▶	460
	La Condamine ▶	
	Jausiers ▶	
	BARCELONNETTE ▶	480

🍴 Refreshments   ⌂ Accommodation   ✚ Hospital/Medical clinic   ✚ Pharmacy
ⓘ Tourist information   ✿ Cycle shop   ⓔ eBike charging   🚉 Rail station

Ride planner from Thonon-les-Bains

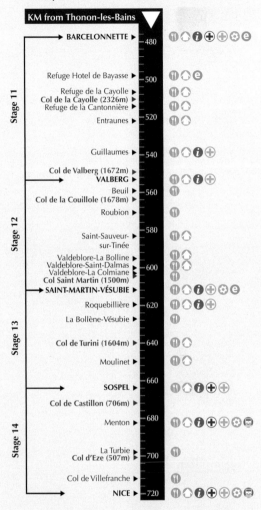

KM from Thonon-les-Bains

Stage 11
- **BARCELONNETTE ▶** — 480 🍴 🏠 ❶ ⊕ ⊕ ☺ ⓔ
- Refuge Hotel de Bayasse ▶ — 500 🍴 🏠 ⓔ
- Refuge de la Cayolle ▶ 🍴 🏠
- **Col de la Cayolle (2326m) ▶** 🍴 🏠
- Refuge de la Cantonnière ▶ 🍴 🏠
- Entraunes ▶ — 520 🍴 🏠
- Guillaumes ▶ — 540 🍴 🏠 ❶ ⊕

Stage 12
- **Col de Valberg (1672m) ▶**
- **VALBERG ▶** 🍴 🏠 ❶ ⊕
- Beuil ▶ — 560 🍴
- **Col de la Couillole (1678m) ▶**
- Roubion ▶ 🍴
- Saint-Sauveur-sur-Tinée ▶ — 580 🍴 🏠
- Valdeblore-La Bolline ▶ 🍴 🏠
- Valdeblore-Saint-Dalmas ▶ — 600 🍴 🏠
- Valdeblore-La Colmiane ▶ 🍴
- **Col Saint Martin (1500m) ▶**
- **SAINT-MARTIN-VÉSUBIE ▶** 🍴 🏠 ❶ ⊕ ☺ ⓔ

Stage 13
- Roquebillière ▶ — 620 🍴 🏠 ❶ ⊕
- La Bollène-Vésubie ▶ 🍴
- **Col de Turini (1604m) ▶** — 640 🍴 🏠
- Moulinet ▶ 🍴 🏠
- **SOSPEL ▶** — 660 🍴 🏠 ❶ ⊕ ⊕

Stage 14
- **Col de Castillon (706m) ▶**
- Menton ▶ — 680 🍴 🏠 ❶ ⊕ ⊕ ☺ 🚉
- La Turbie ▶ — 700 🍴
- **Col d'Eze (507m) ▶**
- Col de Villefranche ▶ 🍴
- **NICE ▶** — 720 🍴 🏠 ❶ ⊕ ⊕ ☺ 🚉

🍴 Refreshments 🏠 Accommodation ⊕ Hospital/Medical clinic ⊕ Pharmacy
❶ Tourist information ☺ Cycle shop ⓔ eBike charging 🚉 Rail station

Main Route Schedule

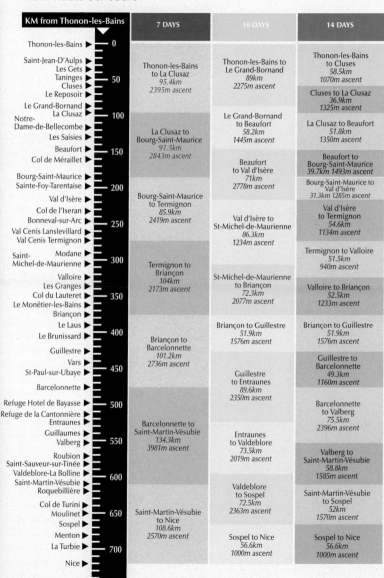

KM from Thonon-les-Bains

Location	KM
Thonon-les-Bains	0
Saint-Jean-D'Aulps	
Les Gets	
Taninges	50
Cluses	
Le Reposoir	
Le Grand-Bornand	
La Clusaz	100
Notre-Dame-de-Bellecombe	
Les Saisies	
Beaufort	150
Col de Méraillet	
Bourg-Saint-Maurice	
Sainte-Foy-Tarentaise	200
Val d'Isère	
Col de l'Iseran	
Bonneval-sur-Arc	250
Val Cenis Lanslevillard	
Val Cenis Termignon	
Modane	300
Saint-Michel-de-Maurienne	
Valloire	
Les Granges	
Col du Lauteret	350
Le Monêtier-les-Bains	
Briançon	
Le Laus	400
Le Brunissard	
Guillestre	
Vars	450
St-Paul-sur-Ubaye	
Barcelonnette	
Refuge Hotel de Bayasse	500
Refuge de la Cantonnière	
Entraunes	
Guillaumes	
Valberg	550
Roubion	
Saint-Sauveur-sur-Tinée	
Valdeblore-La Bolline	600
Saint-Martin-Vésubie	
Roquebillière	
Col de Turini	650
Moulinet	
Sospel	
Menton	
La Turbie	700
Nice	
	750

7 DAYS

Thonon-les-Bains to La Clusaz
95.4km
2395m ascent

La Clusaz to Bourg-Saint-Maurice
91.5km
2843m ascent

Bourg-Saint-Maurice to Termignon
85.9km
2419m ascent

Termignon to Briançon
104km
2173m ascent

Briançon to Barcelonnette
101.2km
2736m ascent

Barcelonnette to Saint-Martin-Vésubie
134.3km
3981m ascent

Saint-Martin-Vésubie to Nice
108.6km
2570m ascent

10 DAYS

Thonon-les-Bains to Le Grand-Bornand
89km
2275m ascent

Le Grand-Bornand to Beaufort
58.2km
1445m ascent

Beaufort to Val d'Isère
71km
2778m ascent

Val d'Isère to St-Michel-de-Maurienne
86.3km
1234m ascent

St-Michel-de-Maurienne to Briançon
72.3km
2077m ascent

Briançon to Guillestre
51.9km
1576m ascent

Guillestre to Entraunes
89.6km
2350m ascent

Entraunes to Valdeblore
73.5km
2019m ascent

Valdeblore to Sospel
72.5km
2363m ascent

Sospel to Nice
56.6km
1000m ascent

14 DAYS

Thonon-les-Bains to Cluses
58.5km
1070m ascent

Cluses to La Clusaz
36.9km
1325m ascent

La Clusaz to Beaufort
51.8km
1350m ascent

Beaufort to Bourg-Saint-Maurice
39.7km 1493m ascent

Bourg-Saint-Maurice to Val d'Isère
31.3km 1285m ascent

Val d'Isère to Termignon
54.6km
1134m ascent

Termignon to Valloire
51.5km
940m ascent

Valloire to Briançon
52.5km
1233m ascent

Briançon to Guillestre
51.9km
1576m ascent

Guillestre to Barcelonnette
49.3km
1160m ascent

Barcelonnette to Valberg
75.5km
2396m ascent

Valberg to Saint-Martin-Vésubie
58.8km
1585m ascent

Saint-Martin-Vésubie to Sospel
52km
1570m ascent

Sospel to Nice
56.6km
1000m ascent

The Col de la Colombière climbs above Le Reposoir (Stage 2)

INTRODUCTION

The views of Mont Blanc are glorious from the summit of the Col des Aravis (Stage 3)

'The Route of the Alps! [...] It is neither that of Hannibal (...) nor that of Bonaparte (...) Our route of the Alps does not threaten the fertile plains of Lombardy and does not facilitate any invasion (...) Its value, for us, is to be the most remarkable tourist route that France can boast of.'
Abel Ballif, president of the Touring Club de France, 1909

Cycling among mountains is a rewarding experience, with a sense of achievement complementing the spectacular scenery that opens up around every turn in the road. The Route des Grandes Alpes (RdGA) is no exception. From the southern shore of Lac Léman to the Mediterranean-licked promenades of cosmopolitan Nice, the 720km route, which Abel Ballif and the Touring Club de France worked hard to make a reality, traverses the inspiring passes of some of France's highest peaks, offering the opportunity to explore a variety of national parks and showcasing the striking contrast between the northern and southern French Alps.

Split into 14 stages with an average distance of 52km, but with a number of alternative route options and itineraries on offer including a seven-day itinerary for the fit cyclist experienced at riding in the mountains, the RdGA provides the perfect Alpine cycling experience. Remember to carefully and realistically consider your fitness and experience levels when selecting your itinerary and allow at least one day either side of

The Col de l'Iseran is the highest paved pass in the French Alps (Stage 6)

your schedule for travel to and from the route. In reality even the seven-day schedule means at least a nine-day break.

Starting in the lakeside town of Thonon-les-Bains, the route visits the Chablais massif before the pastures of the Haute-Savoie come into view. The route winds its way south via the Colombière, Aravis and Saisies passes towards Bourg-Saint-Maurice and the Vanoise National Park. During the route's opening stages, spent under the shadow of Mont Blanc, a 12th-century monastery and the Beaufortain cheese co-operative offer opportunities to spend a few hours off the bike exploring the history and culture of the northern Alps as well as loading up with local produce.

Through the Vanoise the climbing leads to the famous ski resort of Val d'Isère before heading to the Col

On the southern slopes of the Galibier, a monument stands in memory of Henri Desgrange, the founder of the Tour de France (Stage 8)

16

de l'Iseran: at 2770m the highest paved pass in the Alps. It is a daunting undertaking – no wonder Maurice Novarina built a small chapel at the top in 1939.

From the summit of the Iseran the route descends towards the Maurienne valley, to the Écrins National Park and the Col du Galibier – the favourite climb of the founder of the Tour de France, Henri Desgrange. When the Galibier was introduced to the Tour in 1911, Desgrange was moved to write that 'All one can do before this giant is doff one's hat and bow'. The past pedal strokes of the racers of the Tour are never far from you on the RdGA, and a monument to Desgrange now stands on the southern flank of this monstrous mountain.

After the Galibier comes a drop to the Col du Lautaret before the route heads to the Queyras massif via Briançon – designated the highest city in France – and the Col d'Izoard. A descent through the natural cathedral of the Casse Déserte leads to Guillestre. The colourful town of Barcelonnette and the remote Mercantour National Park come next,

Major climbs on the RdGA			
Climb	Altitude	Length	Average gradient
Col des Gets	1170m	7.7km	3.6%
Col de la Colombière	1613m	18.6km	6%
Col des Aravis	1486m	10.1km	5%
Col des Saisies	1650m	15km	4.8%
Le Cormet de Roselend	1967m	23km	6%
Col de l'Iseran	2764m	47.2km	4.2%
Col du Télégraphe	1566m	11.9km	7.2%
Col du Galibier	2642m	18.2km	6.8%
Col d'Izoard	2360m	20km	5.7%
Col de Vars	2108m	19km	6.5%
Col de la Cayolle	2326m	29.1km	4%
Col de Valberg	1672m	12.2km	6%
Col de la Couillole	1678m	7.2km	3.2%
Col Saint Martin	1500m	16.2km	6.4%
Col de Turini	1604m	15.2km	7.2%
Col de Castillon	706m	7km	5.1%
Col d'Èze	507m	17.7km	3.1%

where the spectacular landscape comes complete with a surprising smattering of Mexican-style villas built by immigrants in the late 1800s and early 1900s.

From the wilds of the Mercantour the smell of the Mediterranean soon hangs in the air as the RdGA continues southwards, taking in the switchbacks of the Col de Turini, made famous by the Monte Carlo Rally, to the resort of Menton. It then heads west for a blast along the Cote d'Azur's Grande Corniche to the route's finish on the Promenade des Anglais in Nice.

With over 17,000m of climbing, the route is a celebration of both the natural splendour and the culture of the mountains. It is undoubtedly challenging and not for novices – if you have not ridden extensively in the mountains, it is better to ride individual climbs to hone your abilities before embarking on such a route – but with developing eBike technology and charging facilities now available along the route, it is no longer necessarily the preserve of the ultra-fit. The majesty of the RdGA is opening to a whole new audience.

The RdGA is a popular route with cyclists, motorbikers and car enthusiasts, and certain sections of the route can be busy, most notably the section from Thonon-les-Bains to Beaufort, the famous passes of the Iseran, Galibier and Izoard and the final stretch bordering the coast from Menton to Nice. Because of this the route demands care and attention

The route is popular with motorcyclists as well as cyclists (Stage 6)

– nothing can chill the heart of a cyclist on the tight roads of a mountain pass quite like the roar of a fast-approaching motorbike or sportscar. If possible, it is recommended you avoid undertaking the busier sections of the route at weekends.

Due to its popularity and the frequent visits from the Tour de France, the road surfaces tend to be well maintained. However, it should always be remembered that this is a high-mountain route and, therefore, can present many challenges. In addition, some areas are particularly remote – especially through the Mercantour National Park and on the higher passes. Good preparation is therefore vital to ensure an enjoyable experience.

Aside from the respective start and finish points of Thonon-les-Bains and Nice, the route traverses, or closely passes, a number of towns of interest. On the main RdGA Beaufort, Briançon, Barcelonnette, Sospel and Menton are all attractive places with intriguing histories worthy of exploration should time allow, while Annecy (Variant 1) is one of the jewels of the French Alps.

HISTORY OF THE ROUTE DES GRANDES ALPES

Léon Auscher, vice-president of the mountain tourism committee of the Touring Club de France, the body established to promote cyclo-tourism in France, was one of the first to raise the prospect of developing the road network in the French Alps for the purposes of tourism. Up until that point the existing roads had been built to fulfil the military's need for good links between the Vauban-built forts securing France's Alpine border. Auscher's aim, stated in 1904, was to improve and build upon that infrastructure so tourists could travel among the peaks and enjoy their natural splendour: '… to make possible a direct north–south journey between Evian and Nice, Lake Geneva and the Mediterranean.'

There was widespread support for the project but engineering complexities and funding constraints hampered development. Nevertheless, by 1911 the Paris-Lyon-Méditerranée company was promoting a five-stage trip

through the Alps, from Lac Léman to the Mediterranean. One year later a new national road number – 202 – was classified and dubbed the Route des Alpes, although its completion would be interrupted by war.

One of the main obstacles to the full realisation of the vision was the linking of the Tarentaise and the Maurienne valleys. While Val d'Isère and Bonneval lie either side of the Col de l'Iseran – today just some 30km apart – in the early 1900s to travel between the two by motorable valley roads meant a journey of more than 225km. It was clear that the future success of the entire project rested on the construction of a road that directly linked the two.

Work didn't start on the road over the Iseran until 1929, and it took some 600 workers 6 years to complete what would become the highest paved pass in France. It was officially opened on 10 July 1937 by the President of France: Albert Lebrun. 'It will be the great summer route' reported the newspaper *Excelsior*. 'In the harsh and grandiose landscape, the Iseran road will be criss-crossed by innumerable travellers, who are now allowed to taste the joys of mountaineering without fatigue.'

While the many cyclists who have toiled up the Iseran in the decades since may disagree with that last sentiment, the opening of the road finally brought the reality of Auscher's original vision closer. In 1950 the route was renamed the Route des

Grandes Alpes and some 20 years later the completion of the Cormet de Roselend, linking Beaufort and Bourg-Saint-Maurice, was the final major piece in what is today's main route.

In 2012, the official finish was moved from Menton to Nice, adding a further 37km and bringing the addition of the Col d'Èze, completing the modern-day RdGA.

CONNECTION WITH THE TOUR DE FRANCE

First held in 1903 by the sports daily *L'Auto*, the Tour de France soon developed into cycling's most famous and prestigious race, a position it retains to this day. In 1910 race organisers went in search of new challenges to throw at the riders and added the Pyrenees to the race route. The result was astonishing. Riders were forced from their bikes and on foot they pushed their heavy machines up the steep and unpaved mountain roads, hurling insults at race officials as they passed. Nevertheless, the readers of *L'Auto* lapped up reports of the exploits of the riders in the high mountains, and the experiment was deemed a success. The following year, the high Alps were included in the route for the first time.

Of the climbs on the main RdGA, the Aravis, Télégraphe, Galibier and Castillon featured during the Tour's first

A monument at the top of the Col d'Izoard commemorating the work of those who built the roads that made the RdGA possible (Stage 9)

foray into the high Alps, although it was the monstrous Galibier that most captured people's attention. Émile Georget was the first to scale the Alpine giant, going on to the win the stage in Grenoble. However, the introduction of the Alps did not sit well with the riders and the eventual overall winner, Gustave Garrigou, spoke of the 'tasteless prank of slipping mountains under the roads of our beautiful country'. He went on to say, somewhat tongue in cheek, that during the Galibier stage he had considered Desgrange a 'real assassin to force us to spend our holidays like this'.

More than 100 years since their introduction, the Alps are now one of the cornerstones of the Tour and a race without a number of key Alpine stages is all but unthinkable. It is in the rarefied air of the mountains where Tour de France history is most often crafted and where incredible stories are written, such as Louison Bobet attacking on the Col de Vars in 1953 on his way to the first of three Tour wins, scaling the Col d'Izoard in glorious isolation while being watched by the cycling great Fausto Coppi who was waiting on the mountain with his camera.

The Alps have also played a huge part in women's cycling. While sadly the 2022 reincarnation of the women's Tour de France will not visit the Alpine regions, in its 1980s hey-day the race often brought the female peloton to some of cycling's most storied climbs. In 1989, for example, Jeannie Longo attacked on the Izoard, as Coppi and Bobet had done before her, winning in Briançon on her way to a third straight Tour title.

All of the climbs featured on the RdGA have been included on the Tour de France route, uniquely allowing the tourist to follow in the pedal strokes of cycling legends young and old, male and female.

NATURAL ENVIRONMENT

As well as traversing a number of valleys, mountain chains, regional parks and UNESCO-protected areas, the route encompasses the following designated parks, each with its own unique landscape and wildlife:

Parc national de la Vanoise

Created in 1963, the Vanoise was France's first national park. The core of the park covers 535km², between the Tarentaise and Maurienne valleys, and borders Italy's Gran Paradiso National Park, together forming a protected area of some 1250km², the largest in western Europe. The Vanoise claims over 1700 plant species of which more than 180 have been designated as rare and protected, including 5 species of orchid, 5 species of rock jasmine and 12 species of sedge. As well as chamois, ibex, hares and marmots on the ground, there are some 125 birds that nest in the Vanoise, including golden eagles, eagle owls and the three-toed woodpecker, which, it is claimed, is unique to France and to the Savoie and Haute-Savoie departments.

Parc national des Écrins

Covering a core area of 935km², the Écrins National Park was established in 1973. Encompassing 150 peaks over 3000m and more than 70km² of glacier, its highest point is the 4102m

Often-shy marmots can sometimes be spotted (Stage 6)

The top of the Izoard marks the entry into the Queyras regional park (Stage 9)

Barre des Écrins. The Écrins is punctuated by alpine pastures, grazing cattle and some 410km² of forest, with beech, European larch and Swiss pine trees all found here. Recent sightings of wildlife in the park at the time of writing include the high brown fritillary butterfly, the black yellow owlfly and the European roe deer.

Parc naturel régional du Queyras

Granted regional park status in 1977 and stretching from the community of Abriès-Ristolas in the north to Guillestre in the south, the Queyras regional park covers an area of 610km². The river Guil is the park's main watercourse and is home to brown trout while the Tengmalm (or boreal) owl can be found in the pine forests on the park's high mountain slopes.

Parc national du Mercantour

Wild and desolate, the park saw the return of grey wolves to France in 1992. The Mercantour has been described as nature on steroids and can feel like another world altogether. The core of the park measures 679km² and neighbours Italy's Alpi Marittime protected area. With the 3143m Cime du Gélas, the park's highest point, the Mercantour marks the southernmost point of the Alpine arc before it meets the Mediterranean Sea. It extends into two departments – the Alpes-Maritimes and the Alpes-de-Haute-Provence – and eight distinct valleys. The park claims the greatest diversity

of plants and flowers of any national park in France, with more than 2000 plant species. Of these, 200 are declared rare, including the striking *Saxifraga florulenta*, which was the first emblem of the park when it was established in 1979.

WHEN TO GO

The best times to ride the RdGA are mid June to the end of July and early September to mid October. This avoids the peak summer month of August, when it can get extremely busy and the weather can be unbearably hot, but ensures the passes should all be open (in 2021 the Col du Galibier opened on 11 June). It should be noted, however, that the earlier or later you ride the more likely some passes may be closed at short notice. For reference, the ride to research this guidebook was undertaken across 17 days in late June and early July, and the author experienced extremely hot conditions, including several 40°C days in succession. While all passes remained open during the trip, a hailstorm and subsequent landslide closed the Cormet de Roselend just days after the author's return. This is referenced only to reinforce the necessity of regularly checking the status of passes – see below.

RIDING IN THE MOUNTAINS

There are few better experiences on a bike than gradually winding your way up a mountain road, traversing verdant mountain pastures to a soundtrack of cow bells, while dramatic peaks tower high above you. The sense of achievement as you stand at the summit gazing down at the road you have conquered cannot be overstated.

Nevertheless, riding in the mountains is challenging and careful preparation is fundamental to ensuring you have a positive experience. Below are some key factors to make sure your time riding the RdGA is an enjoyable one.

Understanding the day's route

Make sure you know your route before setting off for the day. The main route is generally well signposted on the road, but it is recommended that you spend time studying the stage descriptions and maps contained within this guide before setting out.

Mountain passes can close at short notice due to road or weather conditions. It is vitally important to check on the day that the passes on the planned route remain open: visit www.cols-cyclisme.com, a good resource for updated information; you can also subscribe to the site's twitter feed @ouverture_cols for regular updates on the status of passes. Stage profiles are offered in the route section of this book as a guide. More detailed profiles of the individual climbs can be found on the RdGA official website: www.routedesgrandesalpes.com/grands-cols. Other resources include individual departments' official traffic websites, which are more detailed but not so convenient to navigate. These

are listed in Appendix C – Useful resources and essential information.

In the event of passes on the main route being closed there are a number of variants available. Detailed guides to the route's main variants are listed in the route section of this book. A summary of options in the event of closed passes is detailed in the following table. Remember to check the status of roads and passes of any alternative route selected.

It is also important to know in advance where there will be opportunities for topping up food and drink supplies or where a repair shop or, for eBikers, a battery-recharging facility can be found. Be aware that in France businesses often shut for lunch, including tourist offices, so check current opening hours and time your visits accordingly. Ski resorts that are packed in winter can resemble ghost towns in spring and summer, meaning cafés or restaurants that you might expect to be open can be shuttered up on arrival, particularly midweek. If you are going to be relying on a mountain café to refuel, it is important that you check before setting off that it will be open, particularly if you are not riding during the peak summer weeks.

Many of the passes include numerous tunnels, some of which are long. Entering these from the bright sunshine of an Alpine summer day can be disorientating, both for the cyclist and the motorist, so the use of high-quality bike lights and reflective

Stage	Closed pass	Alternative route	Passes added
1	Col des Gets (1170m)	(1) From Thonon-les-Bains take D12 south. Traverse Col de Cou/Bonneville/ Glières-Val-de-Borne. Re-join main route at Le Grand Bornand.	Col de Cou (1117m)
2	Col de la Colombière (1613m)	(1) From Thonon-les-Bains take D12 south. Traverse Col de Cou/Bonneville/ Glières-Val-de-Borne. Re-join main route at Le Grand Bornand.	Col de Cou (1117m)
3	Col des Aravis (1486m); Col des Saisies (1650m)	(1) From St-Jean-de-Sixt take Variant 1. (See Variant 1 detailed route). (2) From St-Jean-de-Sixt take Variant 1 to Thônes. At Thônes follow D12 south (later becomes D210C). Re-join Variant 1 at Albertville.	(1) Col de Bluffy (630m); Col de Leschaux (897m); Col du Frêne (950m). (2) N/A
4	Cormet de Roselend (1967m)	(1) From Beaufort take D925 to Albertville. Then D990 south to La Bathie. Then D66 south to junction with D213 to join Variant 2 before ascent of Col de la Madeleine. (See Variant 2 detailed route).	(1) Col de la Madeleine (1993m)
5/6	Col de l'Iseran (2764m)	(1) From Bourg-Saint-Maurice take Variant 2. (See Variant 2 detailed route).	(1) Col de la Madeleine (1993m).
7/8	Col du Télégraphe (1566m); Col du Galibier (2642m).	(1) From Lanslevillard-Val-Cenis take Variant 3. (See Variant 3 detailed route). (2) From Saint-Jean-de-Maurienne take Variant 4. (See Variant 4 detailed route).	(1) Col du Mont-Cenis (2081m); Col de Montgenevre (1850m). (2) Col de la Croix de Fer (2064m)/Col du Glandon (1924m); Col du Lauteret (2058m).
9	Col d'Izoard (2360m)	(1) From Briançon the most direct alternative is to take N94 to Guillestre. The N94 is a busy and fast road and so try to take some of the smaller roads that run parallel where possible: D36/D4/D994E/D138A/D38	(1) N/A
10	Col de Vars (2108m)	(1) From Guillestre take Variant 5. (See Variant 5 detailed route).	N/A

Stage	Closed pass	Alternative route	Passes added
11	Col de la Cayolle (2326m)	(1) From Jausiers take Variant 6. (See Variant 6 detailed route). (2) From Barcelonnette take D908 south towards Colmars. Then D2 and D78. Re-join main route at St-Martin-d'Entraunes.	(1) Col de la Bonette (2715m). (2) Col d'Allos (2250m); Col des Champs (2087m).
12	Col de Valberg (1672m); Col de la Couillole (1678m)	(1) From Jausiers take Variant 6. (See Variant 6 detailed route).	(1) Col de la Bonette (2715m)
13	Col de Turini (1604m)	(1) From St-Martin-Vesubie remain on M2565 to St-Jean-la-Riviere. Then take M19 and follow through Levens and on to Nice.	N/A
14	Col d'Èze (507m)	(1) At Roquebrune-Cap-Martin remain on M6007 – Moyenne Corniche.	N/A

clothing on every stage of the route is essential to remain safe. Please note that only tunnels deemed particularly long or dangerous have been identified with a warning sign on the accompanying maps.

Weather

Weather conditions in the mountains can change rapidly. During the author's research trip, a ride along a 40°C sun-scorched Alpine valley very quickly turned into bone-freezing temperatures, hailstones and torrential rain halfway up a mountain pass. It is therefore vital that you understand the latest local weather forecast and check regularly for updates. A good source for weather forecasts in the mountains is www.yr.no, which is jointly run by the Norwegian Meteorological Institute and the Norwegian Broadcasting Corporation. Go to the search function on the website and enter the full name of the mountain pass you wish to check to get both long-range and detailed hour-by-hour forecasts. Another good resource is France's meteorological service Meteo-France, www.meteofrance.com.

Clothing

With the potential for quickly changing conditions ever present comes the need to ensure adequate clothing is available at all times. Mornings can be cold in the mountains, even in summer, while later in the day a slow, hot ascent will inevitably turn into a fast, cold descent. Multiple thin layers that are easy to remove as both you and the day heat up are recommended to minimise perspiration. You

should always wear a good base layer and ensure you carry gloves, arm and leg warmers, a snood and a gilet. Careful consideration should also be given to carrying a good-quality waterproof jacket and cap at all times – a poor experience descending from Les Deux Alpes in a sudden rainstorm many years ago means that the author is now never without a rainproof jacket when riding in the mountains, regardless of the forecast. Tinted or clear-lensed glasses will keep the wind out of your eyes, while padded cycling shorts help make long hours in the saddle that much more comfortable. Footwear, while important, is a personal choice. Although cleated cycling shoes that affix to pedals are the choice for many due to increased performance, the author prefers non-cleated shoes for comfort. What is important is that the shoe is specifically designed for cycling rather than just a general trainer. Finally, it (almost) goes without saying that a cycling helmet should be worn at all times.

Equipment and maintenance

A remote mountainside is possibly the worst place of all to be stranded with a broken bike and no knowledge of how to make emergency repairs. It is therefore important that the rider understands basic bike maintenance before embarking on the ride. One-day bike maintenance courses are widely available across the country, as are a number of online tutorials.

As mentioned earlier, many of the passes include dark tunnels that have been cut through the mountain, some of which are long. Entering these from bright sunshine can be disorientating, both for the cyclist and the motorist, so the use of high-quality bike lights and reflective clothing is absolutely essential to remain safe.

A checklist of essential cycling equipment is provided in Appendix B – Recommended cycling essentials checklist.

Refuelling

Regular eating and drinking to maintain energy levels while riding is important – halfway up a stiff climb is no place to run out of energy. Make sure that bottles are recharged before they run dry and that you always carry food. Be aware, however, that overeating can be as bad as under-eating. Advice varies but in general carbohydrate intake should be 30–80g per hour of riding or 20–30% of hourly energy expenditure if known. Every rider is different and with the wide choice of gels, energy bars and drinks available today, it is important to find what works best for you before you embark on the route. Good on-bike nutrition advice is available at www.trainright.com.

Riding

Ride at a speed that is comfortable and smooth for you; it is better to ride slowly but continuously than to force the pace and frequently stop and restart. Good pacing is vital as it is important to avoid going anaerobic on a long climb and pushing the body into the red zone. Remember, this is a route

Sweet treats for sale at the top of the Izoard (Stage 9)

Cyclists congregate at the Col du Télégraphe (Stage 7)

to be enjoyed not to be raced. Much advice is available on the perceived benefits of riding at a high cadence and spinning a low gear and riding in or out of the saddle in the mountains. But it is more important to adopt a riding style that feels natural and comfortable for you. Find out what works best for you by riding long uphill stretches before embarking on the route, remembering that many of the Alpine climbs featured on the route average 5–8% gradients with short stretches of up to 10–15%. Depending on fitness levels be prepared to spend two hours or more riding uphill on some of the long climbs featured on the route. Even professional cyclists riding the most technologically advanced bicycles on offer and carrying nothing but themselves generally climb these mountains at speeds between 16–20kph (in 2019, Tour de France winner Egan Bernal, one of the best climbers in the race, reportedly averaged 20.6kph on climbs that included the Galibier and Iseran). You should expect your climbing speed to be significantly slower and factor that in when planning your day's ride. Also, it is important to remember that the higher the climb the less barometric pressure there is, so while the percentage of oxygen in the air doesn't change there is less air density and, consequently, less effective oxygen content in each breath, as detailed below:

Altitude (metres)	Effective oxygen (%)
0	20.9
500	19.6
1000	18.4
1500	17.3
2000	16.3
2500	15.3
3000	14.4

While views at the summit will likely be diverting, try not to remain at the top of a climb for too long. They are often exposed and wind-blasted and it is important not to get cold. It's far better to keep moving or at least find a place out of the wind for a warm drink and enjoy the views from there.

Descending can be as challenging as climbing. Remember to look ahead and to brake smoothly and gently before entering a corner. Some of the descents on the RdGA are particularly long and technical, so it is important to maintain a good level of concentration throughout. Take extra care in wet conditions when the roads can become slippery and slowing distances increase, even if your bike has disc brakes fitted.

BIKE SELECTION AND PREPARATION

The most important thing in selecting a bike for the route is to ensure that you feel comfortable riding for prolonged periods. Due to the length of the route and the demanding terrain, the following types of bikes are worthy of consideration (note: a mountain bike, designed primarily for off-road use, is not recommended).

Road bikes

For seasoned road cyclists used to extended periods of time in the riding position that road racing bikes demand, and who are not carrying a heavy load, road racing bikes are an option, particularly if splitting the route into relatively short stages. Light and agile, built for speed and aerodynamics, they are well suited for riding the long and generally well-surfaced climbs that feature on the route. However, they offer less stable handling than other options and the tyres are usually narrow and slick, which with many technical descents en route is a disadvantage, particularly on wet roads. Many variants are available, ranging from aerodynamic to endurance road bikes; however, those built purely for speed, such as time-trial bikes, are to be avoided.

Touring bikes

Designed for long-distance rides, road touring bikes are heavier than road racing bikes but are sturdier, handle well and are better equipped to carry load. Tyres on a tourer tend to be wider and thicker than on a road bike and while this creates more rolling resistance, it does reduce the potential for punctures and offers better traction when descending. The geometry of a tourer can make for a more upright riding position, with handlebar options that include drop or straight bars. If you choose straight bars, it is a good idea to also fit some ergonomic bar-end extensions for a more comfortable ride.

Gravel bikes

Similar in appearance to road bikes, a gravel bike offers a yet more robust option and is generally considered the most versatile machine available today. While offering much in the way of road bike efficiency, they have a more forgiving geometry and have more heavily treaded tyres offering more grip. With much of the main route generally well surfaced that additional grip and rolling resistance could be a burden most of the time but most welcome when faced with a narrow, rough descent in wet conditions.

eBikes

With demand booming and charging infrastructure increasingly available, an eBike variant of the bikes listed above is now a viable option for tackling the RdGA. The benefit of battery-assisted pedalling on long and steep climbs is obvious; however, there are a number of things to consider when deciding whether an eBike is the correct choice

for your trip – see the separate eBike riding section for more.

Brakes

Whichever type of bike you choose, given the long descents on the route and the potential for poor weather, disc brakes rather than rim brakes are recommended, even if they are harder to maintain. Disc brakes offer better stopping power, are more effective in wet weather and don't heat the rim, which can cause tyre blowouts; benefits which in the author's view outweigh any disadvantages.

Gears

With more than 17,000m of vertical ascent over the RdGA, ensuring your bike has the correct gear ratios for the terrain, your ability and your riding style is important, so it is recommended you get bespoke expert advice. A compact crankset such as 50/34 with a 11–32T cassette is generally considered sufficient; however, a triple crankset, although frowned upon by some, will offer more mid-range gears.

Bike preparation

Whichever type of bike you choose it is imperative that it has been recently serviced by a well-qualified mechanic before you embark on the route. Tyres and brakes should be in perfect condition and it is recommended that new brake discs or pads are fitted as they will undergo significant wear on the route.

Cyclists riding the Col des Aravis (Stage 3)

Bike hire

There are multiple options for bike hire if you wish to avoid travelling to France with your own bike, including many of the shops listed in Appendix A. However, these will require that you return to the same outlet after use. Alternatively, Bcyclet is a cycle-hire company that will deliver and collect rental bikes from multiple locations throughout the Alps and beyond. As a guide, in August 2021 the author received an online quotation for two weeks' hire in September of an Orbea Vector 10 trekking bike with panniers, with collection from Thonon-les-Bains and drop-off at Nice, for €585. See www.bcyclet.com for more.

EBIKE RIDING

Recent improvements in eBike technology and the increasing availability of charging infrastructure along the route mean that an eBike is now a viable option for riding the RdGA. While the benefits of battery-assisted pedalling on a long climb are perhaps obvious, there are some important factors to take into account when considering this choice.

Weight

Due to the battery and motor an eBike weighs significantly more than its conventional equivalent. In researching this book, the author used a Gepida trekking eBike, which has a listed unladen weight of 23.8kg compared with an average touring bike, which weighs 12–15kg. The battery assistance does compensate for some of the additional weight being carried; however, on long climbs the author found little benefit over a conventional bike until higher levels of assistance were selected, increasing the rate of battery drain.

Hub-drive or mid-drive
Hub-drive eBikes are driven by a motor located on the front or rear wheel hub that propels the wheel as soon as the rider pedals. Mid-drive motors are placed between the pedals on the bottom bracket and respond to the force applied through the pedals. Mid-drive motors are considered preferable for long and hilly rides and so are the recommended choice for the RdGA.

Battery
The capacity and charging time of the battery is all important to ensure your schedule is not excessively interrupted by time-consuming battery charging. Battery performance is impacted by many external factors, such as bike weight, ambient temperature, terrain, road surface quality, wind and riding style, and can vary widely. For that reason, detailed battery-performance figures, or eBike ranges, are not offered in this guidebook as they can be significantly misleading. It is better is to learn about your battery's performance as quickly as possible so you can plan your day's riding and select the required level of assistance as efficiently as possible. A 500Wh battery is the absolute minimum that should be considered, with higher capacities desirable.

Charging
Official Bosch recharging stations have been placed along the route and are listed in Appendix A. While every station listed was confirmed as operational at the time of writing, it is important to note that in the author's experience the availability of these stations can change at short notice. For example, when researching this book, the author discovered a station listed as available at a tourist office had been removed, while another listed facility was closed at lunchtime – an otherwise obvious time to recharge. It is recommended, therefore, that if you are going to be wholly reliant on a listed facility for charging your battery midway through the day's riding you should take the time to double-check the facility remains in place as well as the accessible hours – contact details are provided in Appendix A. Aside from the official charging points listed, cafés, restaurants, bike shops and some tourist sites are generally happy to let you recharge a battery when using their facilities – during the author's research trip no such request was refused. Remember, a fully discharged battery of 500Wh can take around 2 hours to recharge to 50% capacity using a 4A standard charger. The final 20% of any recharge takes the longest, so if time is pressing recharge to around 80% capacity during the day and do a full recharge overnight. Make sure you maintain a watchful eye on battery levels alongside an understanding of what is still to come on the route – the author can attest that riding a heavy, battery-depleted eBike on a mountain climb with no recharging options nearby is not a happy place to be.

Riding style

Riding an eBike in demanding terrain requires as efficient a riding style as possible in order to minimise battery usage. Use as low a level of assistance as is comfortable to reserve battery power for tougher sections. Ride fluidly and consistently, avoiding fast starts or sudden increases in effort through the pedals. And remember that long downhill sections can also feature sharp uphill stretches, so it is unwise to plan to fully exhaust your battery at the top of the last climb of the day thinking it is all downhill from that point – it probably won't be.

TOURING OPTIONS

The touring options for riding the RdGA range from riding completely unsupported with no logistical support and carrying all luggage and belongings on the bike, through to fully-supported cycling tours where all accommodation is arranged, support is provided on the road and luggage moved from place to place for you.

Many enjoy the freedom and relative affordability of the former. However, it is important to remember that the RdGA is no small undertaking and is not the route to try self-supported cycle touring for the first time. For the experienced cycle tourists however this will be the option that appeals most. Remember to pack as lightly as reasonably possible, while ensuring you have all necessary equipment and clothing, and to load the bike so that it does not adversely impact handling. Good advice on cycle touring, including tips on packing for long trips, is available at www.cyclinguk.org.

Camping offers an affordable and often enjoyable accommodation option

If you wish to ride in a group or enjoy logistical support on your ride, specialised companies offer accompanied rides, arranging accommodation and transfers and moving luggage from place to place. Among the companies offering such services are Vélorizons, LaRébenne and Bike-Alive. (See Appendix C for contact details.)

A hybrid option is to ride self-supported but arrange for local taxi companies to transport your luggage to and from your overnight accommodation. Alterntively ask a non-cycling companion to join you in a support vehicle – there is much for the motorist to enjoy en route as well as the cyclist.

ACCOMMODATION

There are plentiful hotels, hostels, auberges, refuges, *chambre d'hôtes* (B&Bs) and campsites on or close to the RdGA. Expect to pay upwards from around €45/night for a hotel room or B&B, €20/night for a dorm bed in a hostel and from €10/night for camping. Pre-erected tents and cabins on campsites are widespread and often available out of high season, providing a good option for a comfortable night while keeping costs down and minimising the amount of equipment you need to carry. It is always a good idea to book accommodation at least a day or two ahead, not least to ensure you have a destination secured before you set out for your day's ride, reducing any late-day stress trying to find a spot for the night after a long day in the saddle. More notice is advisable during during late July and August and if the Tour de France is in the area at the time of your visit be aware that hotels and campsites can be booked up months in advance. Appendix

Refreshments await at the auberge at the top of the Col du Mont Cenis (V3)

C – 'Useful resources and essential information' includes a number of helpful websites and organisations when searching for accommodation.

FOOD AND DRINK

As one might expect from a route that traverses the high mountains of France, the regional food offered throughout the RdGA is often hearty fare reflective of the surroundings. In the northern Alps local specialities celebrate the cheeses produced there, including *tartiflette* – a combination of reblochon cheese, potatoes and lardons – as well as *raclette* and *fondue*. Other local delicacies include perch and cured meats. Further south you can find *oreilles d'âne* (donkey's ears), which is actually a gratin made of spinach and either pasta sheets or pancakes, and once you enter the Alpes-Maritimes, nearer the sea, you will find offerings such as *salade niçoise* and *la socca*, a pancake made with chickpea flour.

The Savoie, Haute-Savoie, Isère, Hautes-Alpes and Alpes-Maritimes departments traversed on the route are all good grape-growing regions, each with regional *appellations*. Grapes grown towards the north of the route include jacquère, roussanne and pinot noir, while grenache and cinsault are cultivated in the south.

It is worth remembering that lunch remains the main meal of the day throughout the Alps, and shops and businesses often close around midday for a couple of hours or more. If planning a picnic lunch be sure to stock up before the delis and bakeries close.

GETTING THERE

The start town of the RdGA, Thonon-les-Bains, lies some 35km north-west of the well-connected city of Geneva (Genève in French), with a number of transport options available into the city.

Contact details for all service providers referenced are provided in Appendix C.

Train

Geneva's mainline railway station (simply called Genève or sometimes Genève Cornavin) welcomes regular direct trains from Paris Gare de Lyon. The Eurostar service runs from London St Pancras to Paris Gare du Nord, and you should allow at least 60 minutes for the transfer between the two Paris stations. Alternatively, take the Eurostar from London St Pancras to Lille and then onwards to Geneva – the transfer in Lille will be less onerous but the onward journey will likely involve at least one change.

From Genève Cornavin station trains to Thonon-les-Bains take 60–90 minutes, depending on the service, and often require you to make a connection. Trains to Thonon-les-Bains from Genève-Eaux-Vives station run directly and take around 45 minutes.

Alpine meadows provide a spectacular backdrop (Stage 8)

If travelling with your own bike ensure the services you select will accept your bike and ask if there are any associated charges and packaging requirements. These all differ dependent on the type of service and whether the train is regional or intercity. At the time of writing Eurostar was not accepting bikes so be sure to check for the latest position.

The official website of France's national state-owned railway company, SNCF, is easy to navigate and contains timetable information on all rail options as well as further details on rail travel with your bike, while the website seat61.com is also a good resource for information. Tickets can be purchased through Trainline or Rail Europe.

Air

Geneva airport is well served from multiple international locations by a variety of airlines. Bus and rail connections from the airport into the city run regularly and arriving passengers can take advantage of 80 minutes' worth of free public transport by collecting a ticket in the baggage reclaim area. Private taxis into the city cost between CHF35 to CHF45 (£28–£35).

If opting to travel by air with your own bike be sure to read and fully understand the airline's policy regarding the transportation of bicycles which can normally be found in the 'sporting equipment' section of their website. Exact requirements will vary from airline to airline but all will require the bicycle to be packaged, with pedals detached and handlebars turned inwards. Many will also require partial or full deflation of tyres.

Options for packaging vary from heavy-duty large polythene bags or the cardboard boxes used to deliver new bicycles, through to fabric bags and hard shell bicycle boxes. Each have their own advantages and disadvantages: while hard shell boxed may be considered to offer the best overall protection, they require storage once through the airport which can prove costly for prolonged trips – Geneva airport has baggage storage available for around £10/day for a maximum period of one month. In any case storage may not be practicable if returning home from a different airport. Polythene bags may seemingly offer less protection, though according to CyclingUK there is evidence that bikes are treated better by handlers when the bike is visible, but can be folded down and are light enough to be carried on the bike, or perhaps posted to your final destination for later collection. Indeed in order to ease cycle touring abroad, CyclingUK designed a polythene bag for this purpose. Whatever your chosen packaging medium it is a good idea to protect your bike before – tips include pipe lagging on tubes but cardboard carefully wrapped around the frame and other points of potential damage such as the derailleur can be an equally good and more environmentally friendly option.

Good advice on flying with your bike can be found here: www.cyclinguk.org/cyclists-library/bikes-public-transport/bikes-air. Note that transporting an eBike via a passenger plane is restricted because the lithium battery is classified as a dangerous item and so prohibited. The only option is to send your eBike separately via a freight company.

Bus

A number of companies, such as Flixbus and BlaBlaCar, offer bus travel between major European cities, including London to Paris and Paris to Geneva. The Transalis T71 bus line runs from multiple locations in Geneva to Thonon-les-Bains.

Be aware that many bus companies also prohibit the transport of eBikes. Check with the operator before booking.

Road
From Calais to Thonon-les-Bains it is a little over 850km using the following major roads (distances are approximate): A16 (4km), A26 (260km), A4 (36km), A26 (96km), A5 (93km), A31 (74km), A39 (140km), A40 (112km), D1206 (16km), D903 (21km). SANEF operates the motorways and you should expect to pay around €80 on tolls. Eurotunnel operates the channel tunnel crossing, while P&O and DFDS run ferry services from Dover to Calais.

Private transfer
A number of companies, including Shuttle Direct and Alpine Cab, offer private transfers for both passengers and bikes from multiple locations in Geneva.

GETTING AROUND

If you wish to ride in a group or enjoy logistical support on your ride, specialised companies offer accompanied rides, arranging accommodation and transfers and moving luggage from place to place. Among the companies offering such services are Vélorizons, LaRébenne and Bike-Alive. (See Appendix C for contact details.)

If riding independently pack as lightly as possible to minimise the load carried. Alternatively, local taxi companies can be booked to transport luggage from place to place or ask a

non-cycling companion to join you in a support vehicle – there is much for the motorist to enjoy en route as well as the cyclist.

If undertaking only selected stages of the route, the following stage towns have railway stations for easy access to and from the RdGA:

Thonon-les-Bains (S1); Cluses (S1/2); Annecy (V1); Albertville (V1); Bourg-Saint-Maurice (S4/5, V2); Modane (S3); Saint-Michel-de-Maurienne (S3, V4); Saint-Jean-de-Maurienne (V2/4); Oulx (V3); Briançon (S8/9, V3); Guillestre (S9/10, V5); Embrun (V5); Menton (S14); Nice (S14).

GETTING BACK

Like Geneva, the RdGA finish point of Nice is very well connected. Its main railway station Nice-Ville has 11 departures a day direct into Paris Gare de Lyon. Meanwhile, the city's international airport serves 108 destinations (21 in France and 87 international, including 69 in Europe). For return bus travel see the international bus companies previously referenced.

If returning by car it is a little under 1230km from Nice to Calais via the following major roads (distances are approximate): A8 (186km), A7 (275km), A6 (151km), A31 (114km), A5 (91km), A26 (97km), A4 (36km) A26 (260km), A16 (4km). Expect to pay around €115 in tolls.

SAFETY AND EMERGENCIES

France is generally a safe country to visit, although the usual precautions are necessary. Remain vigilant and lock your bike if you are leaving it unattended for any amount of time and take all valuables with you. Be sure to always ride on the right-hand side of a road unless directed otherwise by signage and be careful at T-junctions and roundabouts, where traffic will approach from your left. Note: the road sign *Cédez le Passage* means Give Way and it is illegal to ride while wearing headphones.

Take care on the Alpine passes and be sure to regularly check local weather forecasts and road conditions. For assistance in an emergency call 112. A complete guide to riding safely and legally in France can be found on the France Government website: www.securite-routiere.gouv.fr/reglementation-liee-aux-modes-de-deplacements/velo/equipements-obligatoires-velo (in French).

Be sure to obtain travel insurance prior to departure and ensure the policy covers all planned activities. Following the UK's exit from the European Union (EU), the European Health Insurance Card (EHIC), which entitles the holder to emergency and essential medical healthcare on the same basis as EU citizens while travelling within the EU, will remain valid until its expiry date, after which it will be replaced by the General Health Insurance Card (GHIC). The new GHIC will offer the same protection as the EHIC within the EU. It should be noted that neither the EHIC nor the GHIC are suitable substitutes for travel insurance.

41

USING THIS GUIDE

For the purposes of this guide the main route has been split into 14 stages. Experienced and conditioned cyclists, those used to riding in the mountains and prepared to spend much of the day in the saddle tackling at least 2 major climbs in a single day, should be able to complete the route in 7–10 days. However, the real joy of this route comes with the ability to stop, look and listen, to truly engage with the spectacular surroundings and enjoy all the Alps has to offer. If time allows, the 14-day schedule, punctuated with a couple of rest days in towns of interest, allows for a more immersive experience. For those with tight schedules and strong legs, alternative itinerary options are presented in 'Alternative schedules' at the beginning of this guide.

Each stage includes an introductory boxed section detailing essential information, including stage start and finish points, stage distance, total metres of ascent and descent and refreshment locations. A summary of each stage is then followed by a detailed route description which provides route directions, highlights, areas of note and cumulative stage distances. Maps and profiles provide details of facilities on offer and an indication of the gradients to be expected, while separate boxed sections provide background information on the various towns and places of interest visited en route.

There are a number of available alternative routes (Variants 1–6) should passes be closed or the rider prefer a different route. Note: Variants 2,3 and 5 are designed to avoid the highest passes and instead use valley roads that are frequently busy with heavy traffic. While all have pleasing stretches, this can lead to a very different experience of riding the route and their use should be carefully considered.

GPX tracks

GPX tracks for the routes in this guidebook are available to download free at www.cicerone.co.uk/1054/GPX. If you have not bought the book through the Cicerone website, or have bought the book without opening an account, please register your purchase in your Cicerone library to access GPX and update information.

A GPS device is an excellent aid to navigation, but you should also carry a map and know how to use it. GPX files are provided in good faith, but in view of the profusion of formats and devices, neither the author nor the publisher accepts responsibility for their use. We provide files in a single standard GPX format that works on most devices and systems, but you may need to convert files to your preferred format using a GPX converter such as gpsvisualizer.com or one of the many other apps and online converters available.

THE ROUTE

STAGE 1

Thonon-les-Bains to Cluses

Start	'Km 0', Hôtel de Ville, Thonon-les-Bains (431m)
Finish	Hôtel de Ville, Cluses (488m)
Distance	58km (36 miles)
Total ascent	1070m
Total descent	1013m
Maximum elevation	1170m
Major passes	Col des Gets (1170m)
Refreshments	Saint-Jean-d'Aulps (25km), Morzine (32km), Les Gets (37km), Taninges (48km)

Starting in the attractive town of Thonon-les-Bains on the southern shore of Lac Léman, the opening stage is a welcome leg warmer ahead of the greater challenges to come. The route heads out of town, crossing the Dranse river and traversing the Chablais region. After threading its way through a wooded gorge towards Morzine and Les Gets, the gently rising road peaks at the Col des Gets, the first classified climb of the route but one of the easiest. A 10km descent leads to Taninges after which a short climb out of the small town is followed by a final drop into bustling Cluses.

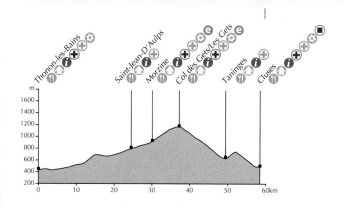

THONON-LES-BAINS

The handsome Hôtel de Ville (town hall) in Thonon-les-Bains was built by Lausanne architects Joseph Mazzone and Louis Perregaud. Work started on the building in 1821, some six years after the 16th-century original was destroyed by a fire caused by the Sardinian soldiers who then inhabited the building. Constructed in the neoclassical style, it took more than 10 years to complete and underwent restoration in the 1960s. The fountain that stands outside dates from 1737 and was sculpted from marble sourced from Vailly.

The town hall stands against a backdrop of the town's attractive marina. Here yachts are moored, ready to cruise the clear waters of Lac Léman, western Europe's largest lake. Formed when the Rhône glacier melted almost 15,000 years ago, Lac Léman has a total surface area of 582km² and a maximum depth of 309.7m. The border between France and Switzerland runs through its centre.

Installed in 2012, the circular bronze plaque attracts cyclists and motorbikers keen for a shot of themselves and their machines at the start of their Alpine adventures.

The RdGA 'Km 0' plaque in the Place de l'Hôtel de Ville in Thonon-les-Bains

Located in the Place de l'Hôtel de Ville is the RdGA 'Km 0' marker that denotes the start of the famous route. ◄

Thonon-les-Bains is a busy working town with all the traffic that comes with a bustling community, so extra care is needed early on when cycling through its streets.

With your back to the front of the Hôtel de Ville and the 'Km 0' marker, turn left onto Rue Michaud, passing the tourist office and the entrance to the funicular on your left.

Opened in 1888 and designed by the engineer Auguste Alesmonières, the **funicular** in Thonon-les-Bains rises 40m and is 230 metres in length. It has an average gradient of 22% and is the only curved funicular in Europe.

Continue along Rue des Ursules and at the roundabout Carrefour du Jet d'Eau take the first exit (SP: Gare SNCF). Continue along Avenue Saint-François de Sales. At the traffic lights turn right onto Avenue Jules Ferry (SP: Gare SNCF). At the roundabout (**0.7km**) take the third exit (not counting the small road signposted 'No Entry') onto Boulevard Georges Andrier. Pass over a level crossing

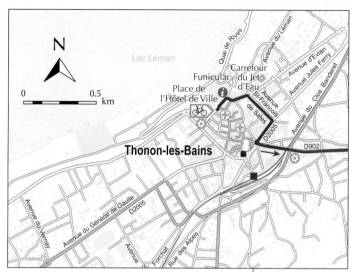

and follow Avenue des Vallées. At the roundabout take the second exit onto Avenue de la Dranse (SP: D902/Morzine/Les Gets).

Exit Thonon-les-Bains (**2.4km**) and take the cycle path over the D1005. Using the cycle path to navigate the busy roundabout take the third exit (SP: D902/Morzine-Avoriaz). The road crosses the **Dranse** (**3.6km**) and then follows the course of the river, flanked by wooded slopes.

The **D902** is a busy road that demands care and attention from the cyclist. With its sweeping bends, it is a popular route with petrolheads and the mountain air can be punctuated by the roar of high-performance super cars. Stay aware and try to avoid starting your journey at the weekend, when the joy-riders tend to emerge in higher numbers. Don't let this put you off – you will experience periods of complete quiet and solitude even this early in the route and things tend to quieten down the further into the high mountains you go.

The Dranse is the first river crossed by the RdGA

Continue towards Morzine, remaining on the D902 at all times. The road rises steadily as it heads towards Le Jotty and Les Gorges du Pont du Diable (**15.5km**).

THE CHABLAIS GEOPARK

The first 35km of this stage takes you through the Chablais, a landscape with a geological history dating back more than 250 million years. With numerous lakes dotting the area, it is well known as a source of mineral water – Évian-les-Bains, home of the famous Evian brand, sits just 10km to the east of the route starting point.

The Chablais is one of 7 designated UNESCO Global Geoparks in France and encompasses 23 geosites that help the visitor to understand the history of the Alps and their formation. Les Gorges du Pont du Diable is one such site, where a stroll through beech trees leads to a series of walkways fixed 50m above the Dranse.

Tourists have visited this gorge since 1893 after a local carpenter, Jean Bochaton, obtained permission to build 'a wooden staircase with iron supports' to access the river. Bochaton continued to develop the site, building more walkways and cutting steps into the limestone. Today some 50,000 visitors come to explore the spectacular gorge annually.

Continue on the D902, descending through cow-grazed meadows. At length pass a left-hand turning to the Abbaye d'Aulps before entering **Saint-Jean-d'Aulps (25km)**.

The **Abbaye d'Aulps** was one of medieval Savoy's most important monasteries and dates from the end of the 11th century. Its ruins were opened to the public in 2007. Exhibitions include an exploration of the link between medicinal plants and monastic heritage.

Continue to the roundabout on the outskirts of **Montriond**. Take the exit signposted 'D902 Morzine/Les

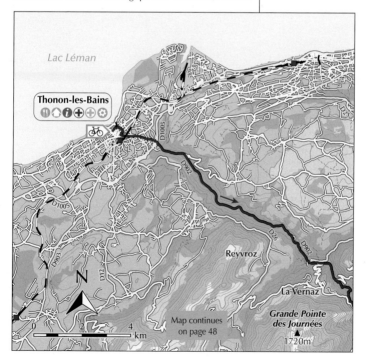

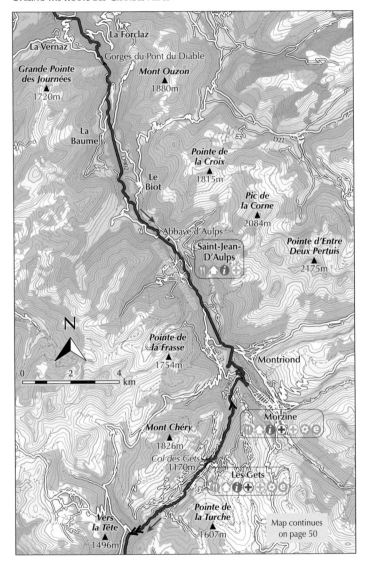

La Forclaz

La Vernaz

Gorges du Pont du Diable

**Grande Pointe
des Journées**
▲
1720m

Mont Ouzon
▲
1880m

La
Baume

D902

**Pointe de
la Croix**
▲
1815m

D22

Le
Biot

**Pic de
la Corne**
▲
2084m

Abbaye d'Aulps

Saint-Jean-
D'Aulps
🍴🏠ℹ️➕

**Pointe d'Entre
Deux Pertuis**
▲
2175m

N

**Pointe de
la Frasse**
▲
1754m

Montriond

0   2   4
km

Morzine
🍴🏠ℹ️➕➕✿🄴

Mont Chéry
▲
1826m

Col des Gets
1170m

Les Gets
🍴🏠ℹ️➕➕✿🄴

**Vers
la Tête**
▲
1496m

**Pointe de
la Turche**
▲
1607m

Map continues
on page 50

Gets' (**29.3km**) and cross the bridge to start the Col des Gets. ▶

The road makes a hairpin to the left and rises steeply through chalets on the outskirts of Morzine. At the next roundabout take the first exit (SP: D902/Les Gets) and continue climbing the chalet-lined road. At the roundabout by the Foyer de Savoie hotel (**32.3km**), take the first exit (SP: D902/Cluses/Les Gets) and complete the climb to the ski station of **Les Gets** (**36.6km**).

> The Col des Gets is a steady and attractive climb. From the bridge over the river Dranse it measures 7.4km at 3.7%.

> **Les Gets** is one of 12 resorts in the Portes du Soleil ski area. Crossing the French Chablais and Swiss Valais regions, the Portes du Soleil is presented as the 'world's oldest cross-border ski destination' and has over 300 marked pistes and 30 snow parks. The region is also a magnet for summer cyclists, with Les Gets one of the area's foremost mountain-biking hubs. The French national team use the resort for training and in 2022 the best mountain bikers in the world will be in town for the UCI Mountain Bike World Championships.

On entering Les Gets, take the first exit at the mini-roundabout (SP: Taninges/Cluses) and traverse the ski resort, passing over three more roundabouts, always following signs for Taninges/Cluses. Exit Les Gets (**39.4km**).

The road now descends through an enjoyable series of steep and sweeping turns as views of high mountains rise into view. At length enter **Taninges** (**48km**).

At the roundabout by the Saint-Jean-Baptiste church take the exit signposted 'D902/Cluses' and exit the town via a long, straight road. After crossing the **Giffre river**, the road climbs offering views over the valley. Pass the intersection with the D4 (**50km**), continuing on the D902. In Châtillon-sur-Cluses go straight over the roundabout by the small pink church (**51.9km**) and exit the village. A fun 5km drop through trees brings you to the edge of Cluses.

At the first roundabout take the second exit (SP: Centre Ville). At the traffic lights turn left onto the Avenue

Flower-filled bikes greet you on entering Cluses

des Alpes (SP: Centre Ville), then cross a railway line and continue into the centre of **Cluses**. Pass the Lycée Charles Poncet and go straight on at the tiny roundabout. The Hôtel de Ville is on the left-hand side, 100 metres further on (**58.2km**).

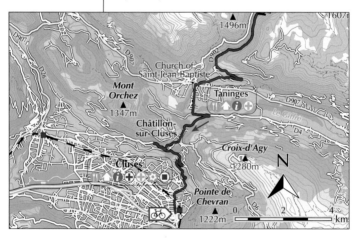

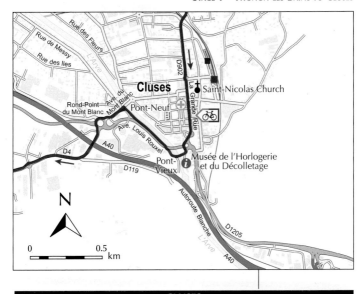

CLUSES

Modern-day Cluses has a population of some 18,000 people and a reputation for precision engineering. This was a predominantly agricultural community until clockmaking was introduced to the Arve valley in 1715 by Claude Joseph Ballaloud. Agricultural workers turned to clockmaking to provide an income during the winter months.

The town's Musée de l'Horlogerie et du Décolletage offers an insight into the history of clock and watchmaking. A state-run clockmaking school was established in the town in 1849, which helped further the capabilities of the town's workers. Over time, clockmaking morphed into the precision engineering technique of turning, with Cluses-based companies now supplying the automotive and aerospace industries. Alongside the timepieces on show in the museum is a selection of early machinery and lathes that enabled precision engineering to grow in the Arve valley.

Cluses' 700 years of history is brought to life on the town's heritage trail, which takes you past 14 places of interest, including the Saint-Nicolas Church, considered the oldest building still standing in the town.

STAGE 2
Cluses to La Clusaz

Start	Hôtel de Ville, Cluses (488m)
Finish	Mini-chalet roundabout, La Clusaz (1071m)
Distance	37km (23 miles)
Total ascent	1325m
Total descent	742m
Maximum elevation	1617m
Major passes	Col de la Colombière (1613m)
Refreshments	Le Reposoir (12km), Col de la Colombière (19.5km), Le Grand-Bornand (30km), Saint-Jean-de-Sixt (33km)

Stage 2 departs Cluses and heads towards the first major climb of the route. Reached via the tiny ski village of Le Reposoir, and guarding the entrance into the Aravis massif, the Col de la Colombière is a very real test of legs and lungs (and for eBikers, battery power). From the top of the Colombière the road descends for 10km to Le Grand-Bornand before kicking up for the final 8km to the charming town of La Clusaz.

Built in 1901 the Hôtel de Ville stands on the site of a former convent. Inside is an electric clock made by the town's students in 1911.

Facing south, with Cluses' Hôtel de Ville on your left, cycle along La Grande Rue. At a small roundabout go straight ahead (second exit) towards the Carrefour de l'Europe roundabout. Go straight over (SP: Office de Tourisme). Turn right onto a cycle path, using the small Pont Vieux stone bridge to cross the **Arve river**. ◄

Turn right after the bridge and continue on the cycle path to the Pont-Neuf. Turn left onto Avenue du Mont Blanc – taking care to observe traffic coming from your left when exiting the cycle path by the Pont-Neuf – and continue to another large roundabout, Rond-Point du Mont Blanc. Take the third exit (SP: D4/Scionzier).

At the roundabout on the outskirts of Scionzier go straight over (second exit). Continue to a second roundabout and take the third exit (SP: D4/Le Reposoir) onto Avenue de la Colombière (**2.2km**).

The Col de la Colombière affords glorious views from its summit

After passing industrial and commercial buildings, the road narrows sharply and care is needed with oncoming traffic. The road gently rises out of Scionzier as you begin the ascent of the Col de la Colombière. ▶

The **Col de la Colombière** first featured on the route of the Tour de France in 1960 when Spain's Fernando Manzaneque led over the pass. It was

From Scionzier the Col de la Colombière is 16.3km at an average of 6.8%. Its maximum gradient is 12% and comes in the final kilometre.

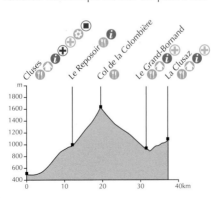

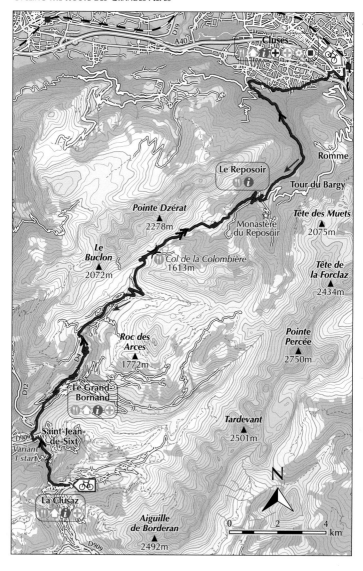

eight years before the climb was used again. Then Britain's Barry Hoban, a rider more suited to flat terrain, escaped the bunch to pick up intermediate sprint points before continuing to scale three Alpine climbs alone to win the stage. His lead over the Colombière that day was some six minutes.

The Colombière rises sharply for 4km, after you pass through the tiny commune of Blanzy, followed by 3km of respite as you approach **Le Reposoir** and emerge into open pasture. Continue on the D4 and exit the village (**12.5km**).

MONASTÈRE DU REPOSOIR

Situated just 1km south of Le Reposoir stands the impressive Monastère du Carmel du Reposoir. In 1151 a chartreuse (Carthusian monastery) was founded on the site under Prior Jean d'Espagne. For nearly seven centuries Carthusian monks lived and prayed beneath the 2750m Pointe Percée, the highest peak in the Aravis range. The French Revolution compelled the monks to leave in 1793 but they returned in 1846.

After falling into disrepair, the monastery was bought in 1922 by Mère Marie de Jésus, who wanted to establish a Carmel in the mountains – a Carmel originally being a convent and home to followers of the Prophet Elijah, who lived in Palestine, near Mount Carmel, in around 900BC. After years of restoration work the Carmel du Reposoir was founded in October 1932. Sadly, Mother Marie didn't live to see the completion of her work. Today the Carmel houses some 18 Carmelites who follow a life of prayer, meditation and work – 'to earn one's bread and not be a burden to anyone'.

From Le Reposoir the road steepens. This is a climb with a sting in its tail and its toughest section comes in the final 3km, where the average gradient is 10%. The reward at the top of the **Col de la Colombière** (**19.5km**) is a bar and restaurant with a south-facing terrace and views of the peaks of the Bargy and Aravis mountain chains.

From the top of the pass descend for 10km through Le Chinaillon to the small but busy town of **Le Grand-Bornand** (**30km**). There are a number of tight bends on the descent so exercise care.

The town of Le Grand-Bornand as seen from Saint-Jean-de-Sixt

In summer **Le Grand-Bornand** hosts the annual Au Bonheur des Mômes youth festival, bringing six days of performing art workshops, exhibitions and shows to the town and attracting some 90,000 festival goers.

At a tight left hairpin before entering the centre of the town, take the turning on the right to continue straight on (SP: Annecy) rather than going around the hairpin. Follow the small road to a mini-roundabout and take the first exit (SP: Annecy/Bonneville) to rejoin the D4 (**31.3km**).

Remaining on the D4, cross the Borne river and enter **Saint-Jean-de-Sixt** (**33.5km**). At the roundabout by the tourist office take the third exit onto the D909 (SP: La Clusaz). ◄

To follow Variant 1 take the first exit at the roundabout by the tourist office in Saint-Jean-de-Sixt (SP: D909/Thônes/Annecy).

Exit Saint-Jean-de-Sixt and start the climb of the Col des Aravis before entering **La Clusaz** (**36.2km**). At the first roundabout take the second exit (SP: Office de Tourisme/Vallée des Aravis). At the next roundabout again take the second exit (SP: Aravis/Confins) into a one-way system at the top of which is a roundabout with a mini chalet in its centre, the end of the stage (**37km**).

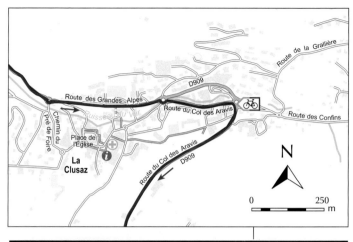

LA CLUSAZ

Home to Guy Périllat who won the fabled Wengen/Kitzbuhel downhill ski-ing double in 1961, La Clusaz has hosted snow sports competitions since the early 1900s, when a road from Annecy opened the area to a new breed of adventure hunters. The first ski competition was organised in 1907 and the first cable car opened in 1956. Today, the town earns its main living from the tourists that come year after year to enjoy the skiing and snowboarding on offer within the Aravis mountain range.

Derived from the word 'cluse', meaning a 'passage between two mountains,' La Clusaz is also a centre for reblochon. Around 20 farms in the area still produce the soft cheese which is a principal ingredient in *tartiflette*, a Savoyard speciality that combines potatoes, lardons and onions and which is found in virtually every restaurant in these parts.

STAGE 3

La Clusaz to Beaufort

Start	Mini-chalet roundabout, La Clusaz (1071m)
Finish	Town centre, Beaufort (738m)
Distance	51.75km (32 miles)
Total ascent	1350m
Total descent	1683m
Maximum elevation	1660m
Major passes	Col des Aravis (1486m); Col des Saisies (1650m)
Refreshments	Col des Aravis (7km), Notre-Dame-de-Bellecombe (22.5km), Les Saisies (34.5km)

The Col des Aravis is an attractive and relatively straightforward opening to Stage 3, with the summit of the pass offering splendid views of Mont Blanc. After crossing the border from Haute-Savoie into Savoie, the route descends to Flumet before kicking up towards Notre-Dame-de-Bellecombe, bound for the second classified climb of the stage – the more difficult Col des Saisies. An enjoyable 15km descent off the Saisies and a relatively flat 3km into Beaufort completes the stage.

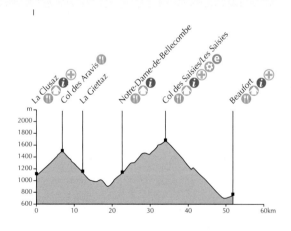

The small Sainte Anne chapel sits at the top of the Col des Aravis

From the mini-chalet roundabout in La Clusaz, where the preceding stage finished, take the D909 exit (SP: Manigod/Col des Aravis), passing chalets and ski lifts before exiting the town (**1.25km**). Remain on the D909 to the summit of the **Col des Aravis** (**7km**) through a series of hairpins, enjoying the spectacular scenery as Mont Blanc rises into view. ▶

From the Stage 3 start point the Col des Aravis is 7km at an average of 5.9%. The maximum gradient is 8.6%.

The top of the **Col des Aravis** denotes the border between the Haute-Savoie and Savoie departments. As well as a couple of restaurants and a gift shop there is a small chapel dedicated to Sainte Anne, patron saint of travellers. Initially constructed in 1650, the chapel was rebuilt in the 1760s by the priest of La Giettaz, a commune some 5km below the pass.

From the top of the Col des Aravis descend through the ski station of **La Giettaz**, passing through tunnels as the road hugs the rockface. Remain on the D909 to Flumet (**18.5km**). Pass the *mairie* and at the next junction turn right (SP: Toutes Directions) to enter a one-way system. Pass the

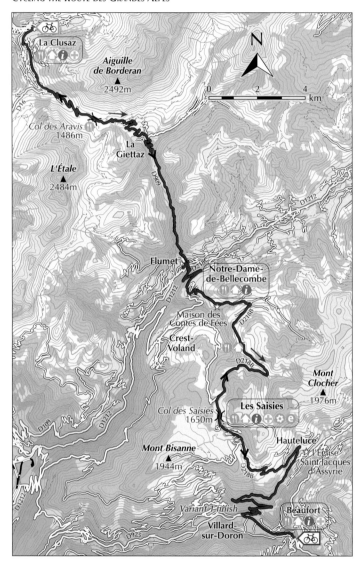

post office and at the mini-roundabout by the tourist office take the third exit onto Rue du Mont Blanc (SP: Chamonix/ Les Saisies). Climb through the town and by the church turn right over a small bridge (SP: D218C/Notre-Dame-de-Bellecombe/Les Saisies). Exit Flumet (**19.5km**).

From Flumet the Col des Saisies is 14.8km at an average of 5%. There is one short section over 10%.

After 2km turn right at the T-junction (SP: D218B/Les Saisies) and climb through **Notre-Dame-de-Bellecombe** bound for Les Saisies. ▸

Situated just beyond Notre-Dame-de-Bellecombe on the D218B is the **Maison des Contes de Fées**. Celebrating the fairy tales of childhood, the museum depicts well-known characters and scenes with lights and animation. Favourites such as Goldilocks and Little red Riding Hood are featured.

The climb to Les Saisies undulates, with the road sometimes flattening or descending for a kilometre or more through Alpine meadows. Pass under a wooden bridge to enter the **Les Saisies** (**34.5km**). Pass over two roundabouts and under another bridge as the road starts to descend through shops and restaurants, passing the tourist office on your right. Proceed straight over two further roundabouts to exit the town (**35.5km**), continuing on the D218B and following signs for Beaufort for a pleasant descent off the Saisies.

A small iron cross stands on the climb of the Col des Saisies

ÉGLISE SAINT JACQUES D'ASSYRIE

Some 7km into the descent of the Saisies is a turning to the left (SP: D70/Col du Joly). A 1km detour down this road will lead to the village of Hauteluce (1km) and the remarkable l'église Saint Jacques d'Assyrie. The church is dedicated to the first bishop of Tarentaise who is understood to have arrived in the valley in the middle of the 5th century to preach to the local population.

Built between 1666 and 1672, the baroque church is notable for its painted façade and a 55m-high bulb steeple. Constructed in the Savoyard style, the steeple is considered to be among the best examples of such architecture in the region. It was razed to the ground in 1794 during the French Revolution. Work on its reconstruction started in 1825 and took five years.

Among the statues and sculptures housed in the church are four intricately carved depictions of saints which adorn the 18th-century walnut pulpit, including one of Saint Jacques d'Assyrie himself. The pulpit is classified as an historic monument and is credited as the work of Jacques Clerant, a sculptor from Moûtiers.

Shortly after traversing the hamlet of La Pierre (**49km**), the road ends by the Hotel Restaurant La Cascade (also the end point of Variant 1). At the junction turn left onto the D925 (SP: Beaufort). Follow the broadly straight road alongside the Doron river before entering attractive **Beaufort**. Pass over two roundabouts, heading to the centre of town. The stage end point is just beyond the second roundabout, alongside a small wooden, covered footbridge that crosses the Doron (**51.7km**).

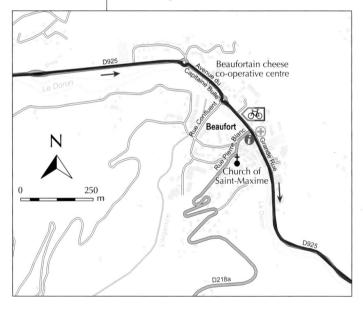

BEAUFORT

The covered footbridge in Beaufort is the end of Stage 3

Beaufort is a small and attractive town – its name combines the French words for 'beautiful' and 'strong' – and it is the main commune of the Beaufortain, a region extending to some 27,000 hectares and encompassing several lakes constructed high in the surrounding mountains to feed hydroelectricity generation.

A meander through Beaufort's pleasant streets is recommended. The Doron flows through the town and there are a number of attractive bridges spanning the river. There are also some buildings of minor historical interest, such as the old imperial gendarmerie, located next to the church of Saint-Maxime de Beaufort.

Beaufort is well known for its eponymous cheese, which is made using milk produced by the brown and white Abondance cows that graze the Beaufortain mountain pastures in summer. It is protected by the Appellation d'Origine Protégée designation, which means only cheese made here can carry the Beaufort label. In 1961, with Beaufort production threatened by industrialisation and an exodus of workers to urban areas, a co-operative of local farmers was founded to share resources and protect production. Today the co-operative has 184 members and produces some 30,000 wheels of cheese annually. The co-operative has a visitors' centre on the Avenue du Capitaine Bulle and it also offers guided tours of the maturing cellars.

STAGE 4

Beaufort to Bourg-Saint-Maurice

Start	Town centre, Beaufort (738m)
Finish	Rond-Point des Grands Cols, Bourg-Saint-Maurice (815m)
Distance	39.5km (24½ miles)
Total ascent	1495m
Total descent	1418m
Maximum elevation	1974m
Major passes	Le Cormet de Roselend (1967m)
Refreshments	Col de Méraillet (12.5km), Refuge du Plan de la Lai (17.5km)

The main feature of Stage 4 is the climb of the Cormet de Roselend via the Col de Méraillet. This one-two combination represents the route's toughest test so far, and the rewarding views that can be enjoyed as the summit nears are hard-earned. The following descent is demanding in places, with the drop into Bourg-Saint-Maurice and the Tarentaise valley among the most technical stretches of the route encountered so far.

From Beaufort the climb to the summit of the Cormet de Roselend via the Col de Méraillet is 20.3km at an average of 6%.

Starting in the centre of Beaufort where the preceding stage finished, with the small wooden footbridge on your right, proceed straight on following signs for Bourg-Saint-Maurice and the Cormet de Roselend. Pass the tourist office on your right and continue straight on through the town, passing shops, restaurants and chalets before exiting the town (**0.5km**) to begin the climb to the Cormet de Roselend. ◄

Some 5km south of Beaufort is the small ski station of **Arêches-Beaufort**, home to the Pierre Menta, an international ski mountaineering competition. Taking its name from the distinctive 2714m peak that dominates the Beaufortain massif, the competition hosts some 400 athletes each year, who take

The summit of the Cormet de Roselend, where the D925 becomes the D902

part in teams of two and scale more than 10,000m over 4 days of racing.

The route follows the Doron river through verdant woods and towering rock as the road rises and the gradient starts to bite. A series of hairpin bends are navigated as the climb opens up towards the Col de Méraillet (**12.5km**). ▶

An alternative route to the Col de Méraillet from Beaufort is via the attractive but steep Col du Pré (12.6km at 7.7%) and the Barrage de Roselend – total 17.8km.

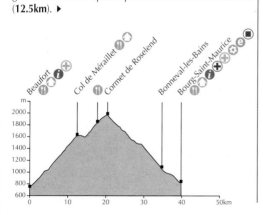

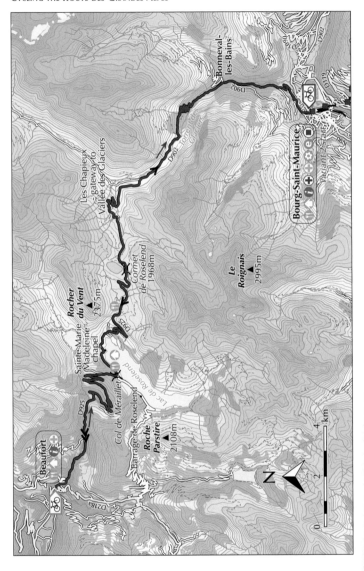

From the **Col de Méraillet** remain on the D925 (SP: Cormet de Roselend), passing the Chalet de Roselend hotel and restaurant – a good option for refuelling and enjoying views over the Roselend lake. A short descent around the northern tip of the lake offers the opportunity for some brief respite, passing a small chapel dedicated to Sainte-Marie-Madeleine, before the road rises sharply once again. For nearly 5km the road climbs steeply before the final kilometre flattens to a relatively benign gradient as you reach the top of the **Cormet de Roselend** (**20.5km**).

The seemingly impossibly turquoise **Lac de Roseland** was created after some 2600 workers built the dam that today lies on its western edge. Work started on the 804m-long and 150m-high dam in 1955 and took 7 years to complete. At 1600m it is the fourth highest dam in France and the lake feeds the hydro-electric plant at La Bâthie. In 1960 the hamlet of Roselend was flooded as a consequence of the work. The Sainte-Marie-Madeleine chapel, which had served the hamlet's population for centuries before the flooding, was rebuilt two years later. Today it stands alongside the road which runs past the lake.

The Chalet de Roselend offers wonderful views over the Lac de Roseland

VALLÉE DES GLACIERS

Just over 6km into the descent of the Cormet de Roselend a left-hand turning (SP: Les Chapieux) takes you to the entry point for the Vallée des Glaciers. From the hamlet of Les Chapieux there is the option to take a two-day hiking excursion from the Auberge de la Nova, a hostel and restaurant that housed some of those who worked on the Roselend dam in the 1950s.

The hiking route is a serious undertaking and should only be tackled by experienced and well-conditioned mountain hikers who are well equipped for all eventualities – never undertake the route alone, understand the weather conditions and know your limits warns the tourist office's leaflet detailing the route. It encompasses a number of passes over 2500m and bypasses several glaciers, meaning areas may still be covered in snow even in summer. There is nearly 2500m of vertical ascent over the 2 days, with the total walking time estimated at 15 hours. Refuge Robert Blanc, which is perched high on a rock at 2760m above the route of the Tour du Mont Blanc, is the one-night stopover.

If that all sounds too demanding but a walk in the mountains still appeals, continue on the bike from Les Chapieux to the car park at Le Ville des Glaciers – or take the small bus that takes visitors between the two – where a 90-minute circular walk heads off on the Tour du Mont Blanc path, continues to the Chalet des Mottets, at the foot of the Aiguille des Glaciers and the Col de la Seigne, and returns via a path the other side of the Torrent des Glaciers.

The Tarentaise is a glacial valley through which the Isère river flows. From its source the river runs for 80km to Albertville in a north-west/south-west/north-west orientation.

From the Cormet de Roselend the road becomes the D902 and descends for 20km to Bourg-Saint-Maurice and the Tarentaise valley. ◀

The descent is steep and tight in places, with a number of technical hairpins and S-bends demanding extra attention. The road follows the route of the Torrent des Glaciers, which offers frequent blasts of cooling air when the meltwater tumbling off the mountain is in full flow.

Enter the hamlet of **Bonneval-les-Bains** (**34km**) and continue on the tree-lined D902 into **Bourg-Saint-Maurice**. The first roundabout you come to is the busy Rond-Point des Grandes Cols and the finish of the stage (**39.5km**).

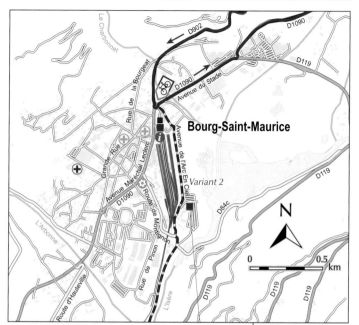

BOURG-SAINT-MAURICE

Home to 8000 locals, Bourg-Saint-Maurice is a centre for outdoor living with many of the benefits a large tourist resort brings. What it lacks in charm it makes up for in convenience. Accommodation is easy to find and there are numerous restaurants and shops. There is also a train station that links with towns to the west through the Tarentaise valley (Bourg-Saint-Maurice being the last stop heading east). It all adds up to an easy place to stay for a day or two to draw breath.

That's not to say the town is purely functional. Dubbed the capital of Haute-Tarentaise and located at the feet of three monstrous Alpine passes – the Cormet de Roselend, the Col du Petit Saint-Bernard and the Col de l'Iseran – it is an important location for many mountain sports, including hiking and white-water canoeing, should some time away from the bike appeal.

As well as the start point for Stage 5, Bourg-Saint-Maurice is also where Variant 2 starts if the Col de l'Iseran is closed.

STAGE 5
Bourg-Saint-Maurice to Val d'Isère

Start	Rond-Point des Grands Cols, Bourg-Saint-Maurice (815m)
Finish	Tourist office, Val d'Isère (1837m)
Distance	31.25km (19½ miles)
Total ascent	1285m
Total descent	263m
Maximum elevation	1837m
Major passes	N/A
Refreshments	Séez (3km), Sainte-Foy-Tarentaise (11.5km)

From the busy town of Bourg-Saint-Maurice to the world-famous ski resort of Val d'Isère, Stage 5 may be the shortest of the entire route but with 15km of the 31km stage sharply uphill, and with little in the way of descent, it is no less demanding. After a simple opening, where the biggest challenge is navigating the traffic of Bourg-Saint-Maurice, the road finally tips upwards, steepening through and beyond Sainte-Foy-Tarentaise as the Col de l'Iseran starts in earnest. The road passes through a number of avalanche tunnels, some of which are long and dark and consequently unpleasant to ride, demanding great care. The road flattens and falls after the Lac du Chevril before arriving in Val d'Isère.

Bourg-Saint-Maurice to the Col d'Iseran measures 48km at an average of 4.1%. Val d'Isère, the end point of Stage 5, lies some 16.5km below the pass.

From the Rond-Point des Grandes Cols take the exit sign-posted D1090/Séez/Val d'Isère onto Avenue du Stade. At the Rond-Point des Arcs by the Intermarché supermarket, take the second exit (SP: D1090/Séez/Col de l'Iseran). Exit Bourg-Saint-Maurice (**1km**). ◄

At the roundabout shortly after entering **Séez** go straight on (SP: D1090/Ste-Foy-Tarentaise/Val d'Isère). Ride through the town and at the next roundabout leave the D1090, which heads towards Italy via the Col du Petit Saint-Bernard, by taking the first exit (SP: D902/Ste-Foy-Tarentaise/Val d'Isère). Exit Séez (**3km**).

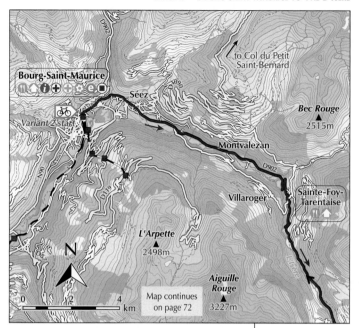

If time and legs allow the 31km climb to the **Col du Petit Saint-Bernard** and the border with Italy is worth the diversion for great views over the Tarentaise valley. The ascent is long but not steep – the average is just 4.4% – and passes through the ski station of La Rosière.

The D902 road descends out of Séez and flattens before kicking up sharply after a bridge over the Sassière stream (**10km**). The road now hairpins upwards towards **Sainte-Foy-Tarentaise**, climbing steeply through the town and

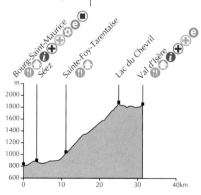

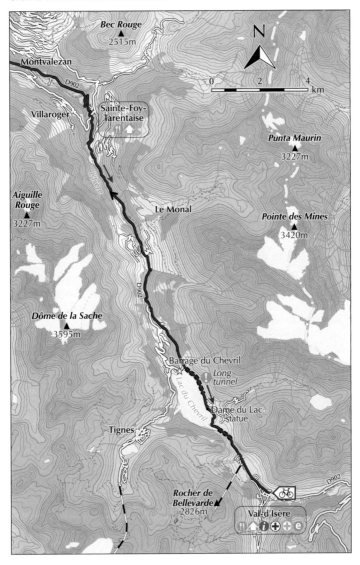

beyond. As the climb progresses, it passes through a number of avalanche tunnels, over which glacial water sometimes pours in summer, and some of which are lengthy.

Perched to the east of the D902 is the hamlet of **Le Monal**. This collection of mountain chalets, which have been preserved since the 18th and 19th centuries, is considered a perfect example of a traditional Haute-Tarentaise village. Le Monal also enjoys perfect views across to the 3779m Mont Pourri and its impressive glacier.

At the Barrage du Chevril (**24km**) remain on the D902 by keeping left and ignoring the right-hand turning

The Barrage du Chevril is the tallest dam in France

The Dame du Lac statue gazes over the Lac du Chevril in memory of the old village of Tignes

At 181m high the Barrage du Chevril is the tallest dam in France. Commissioned in 1953, it is 43.6m thick at its base and retains up to 235m³ of water.

to Tignes – unless you want to add the 6.5km climb to the ski station's car park (a dead end) to your day's riding. Pass the **Lac du Chevril**, taking great care through a number of very dark tunnels that border it, including one which is 1.3km in length. ◄

Exit Le Villaret du Nial, passing an affecting statue of a woman respectfully gazing out over the lake (**26.5km**). Remain on the D902 to enter the outskirts of the drawn-out resort of Val d'Isère (**29km**).

> The **Dame du Lac** statue was erected in memory of the old village of Tignes which was flooded in the creation of the lake to provide hydroelectric power. Some 473 villagers put up a fierce battle against the State but ultimately all were forced to vacate their homes in April 1952. When the village's war memorial was dismantled, a villager reportedly cried, 'You should be ashamed to be French … read on this monument to the dead the names of all our men who gave their blood for this land from which you are chasing us today!'

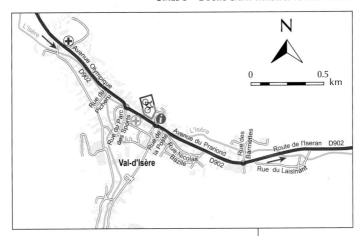

Continue for a further 2km into **Val d'Isère** proper. Proceed straight on at the roundabouts, always remaining on the D902. The resort's tourist office, and the end point of the stage, is on the left just as the Avenue Olympique becomes the Avenue du Prariond (**31.2km**).

VAL D'ISÈRE

Evidence of human inhabitation in the Val d'Isère area extends back to the Celtic tribes who are thought to have been the first to live here, developing agricultural practices and rearing livestock. Centuries later, with Catholicism having taken hold, the village was granted independence from the parish of Tignes by the Pope in 1637. The villagers built their own church seven years later.

Tourism started in the valley in 1888 when L'Hôtel Parisien opened its doors. Nearly 50 years later the village began its move into ski tourism, opening ski schools and building the first lifts. The road from Tignes arrived in 1937 – previously, visitors had to walk to the resort – and Val d'Isère's path to becoming a ski resort of international repute was literally set. By 1956 the town claimed 36 hotels. Fast forward 36 years and its reputation as a premier skiing venue was such that in 1992 it hosted the Olympic downhill race.

Today the resort claims some 27,000 tourist beds and 2 million overnight stays during the winter season as well as some 300km of prepared pistes.

STAGE 6
Val d'Isère to Val Cenis Termignon

Start	Tourist office, Val d'Isère (1837m)
Finish	Maison de la Vanoise, Val Cenis Termignon (1299m)
Distance	54.5km (34 miles)
Total ascent	1125m
Total descent	1663m
Maximum elevation	2764m
Major passes	Col de l'Iseran (2764m)
Refreshments	Col de l'Iseran (16km), Bonneval-sur-Arc (29.5km), Bessans (36.5km), Val Cenis Lanslevillard (46km), Val Cenis Lanslebourg (48.5km)

Traversing the Vanoise national park, Stage 6 leaves Val d'Isère and heads to the Col de l'Iseran, the highest paved mountain pass in the French Alps and where skiers on the Pisaillas glacier can be spotted even in summer. After a climb that is heavy on the legs and demanding on the lungs, there follows a sometimes-technical descent to attractive Bonneval-sur-Arc and the entrance to the Maurienne valley. An enjoyable ride alongside the Arc river and through the villages of Val Cenis brings you to the stage's end point in the village of Val Cenis Termignon.

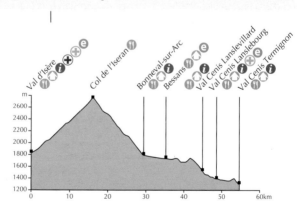

With Val d'Isère's tourist office on your left, cross the roundabout to proceed onto Avenue du Prariond. Go straight on to exit Val d'Isère (**0.75km**). The road out of town is long and broadly straight. It gently rises for 4.5km before passing through Le Fornet and crossing the Isère river via a small stone bridge. ▶

The road now narrows and climbs through a series of hairpins. Very soon the air gets thinner, bringing with it a real feeling of riding high in the mountains. This is the first time the route exceeds 2000m in elevation.

First used by the Tour de France in 1938, the **Col de l'Iseran** has been used by the race sparingly, yet it is etched in Tour history, and not only because of its scale. In 1959 the French darling and three-time winner Louison Bobet ended his Tour de France story on the Iseran, climbing off his bike at the summit on Bastille Day, defeated by the mountain. A photograph captured the moment he walked away from the race that had in many ways defined him, a coat thrown over his shoulders and the Tour's doctor at his side.

The Isère river rises in the Graian Alps and merges with the Rhône river north of Valence, passing through the Drôme, Isère and Savoie departments during its 286km-long course.

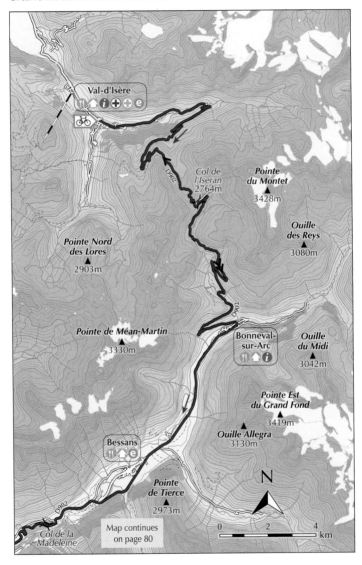

Val-d'Isère

Col de l'Iseran 2764m

Pointe du Montet 3428m

Ouille des Reys 3080m

Pointe Nord des Lores 2903m

Pointe de Méan-Martin 3330m

Bonneval-sur-Arc

Ouille du Midi 3042m

Pointe Est du Grand Fond 3419m

Ouille Allegra 3130m

Bessans

Pointe de Tierce 2973m

Col de la Madeleine

Map continues on page 80

N

0   2   4 km

The road continues through the treeline and the magnitude and exposure of the Iseran becomes apparent. The steep drops from the roadside and the view back down the valley to Val d'Isère, now far below, evidence of how high the road has climbed. Snowbanks are now likely to line the route, even in early summer. The last couple of kilometres kick up sharply before you finally reach the top of the pass with its small chapel, café and views over the descent to come (**16km**).

From the top of the **Col de l'Iseran** there follows a steep and technical descent of some 13km to the diverting village of Bonneval-sur-Arc. Care is needed but do take time to enjoy some of the striking views on offer as the road descends through pillars of rock, crosses little stone bridges and passes torrents of meltwater plunging from the mountain.

Bonneval-sur-Arc is a member of l'association Les Plus Beaux Villages de France

Part of the Plus Beaux Villages de France association, **Bonneval-sur-Arc** marks the entrance of the RdGA into the Maurienne valley. Aside from the narrow streets and stone houses, which are reason enough to stop, attractions include a museum detailing Bonneval's history of mountaineering, a handsome church and the hamlet of Ecot – at 2000m, claimed as the highest village in the valley. A small collection of preserved mountain houses and a protected site since the 1970s, Ecot boasts a chapel with frescoes dating from the Middle Ages and was the venue for the 2013 film *Belle et Sébastien*.

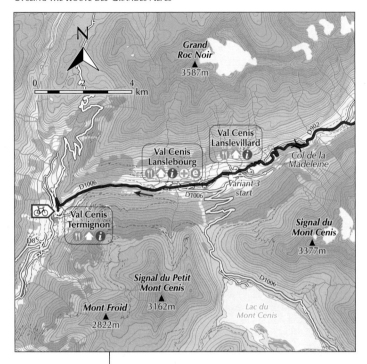

At just 2km this is a different Col de la Madeleine to the long and difficult climb tackled during Variant 2. ◄

From **Bonneval-sur-Arc** (**29.5km**) remain on the D902 which now descends more steadily for another 25km, bar a very short section of climbing to the Col de la Madeleine (**41.5km**), following the Arc river through Bessans and Val Cenis Lanslevillard. ◄

Traverse the drawn-out resort of **Val Cenis Lanslevillard**, always remaining on the D902. At the roundabout at the far end of town take the second exit – not counting the entrance to the car park – (SP: D902/ Lanslebourg).

Val Cenis Lanslevillard is the start point for Variant 3, which climbs the Col du Mont Cenis. While this variant should be avoided unless absolutely necessary – see Variant 3 for more information – the ride to the Col du Mont Cenis is in itself a delight. It is here that some claim Hannibal led some 37 elephants and 60,000 men over the Alps in 218BC (others point to different passes as more likely crossing points). Regardless of where Hannibal and his elephants actually trod, the relatively straightforward climb is worth the effort if time permits.

Take the left-hand turning by the Hotel L'Etoile des Neiges in Val Cenis Lanslevillard (SP: D115/Col du Mont Cenis) to meet the D1006 and then follow to the Col. Retrace your pedal strokes to return to the main route, remaining on the D1006 all the way to Lanslebourg.

Cross the Arc river and enter **Val Cenis Lanslebourg** (**47.5km**). Go straight on at the first roundabout (SP: D1006/Termignon) as the D902 ends and becomes the D1006. Remain on the D1006 for 6km to **Val Cenis Termignon**, which will come into view after a tight

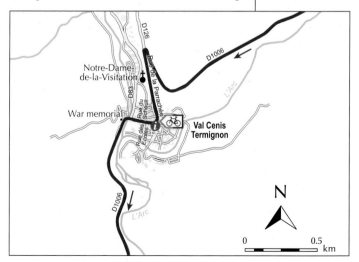

Flower-filled meadows border the valley roads through the Maurienne

left-hand hairpin (**54km**). The stage finish is at the Maison de la Vanoise and tourist office, which is found on the left just as you round a right-hand bend shortly after entering the village (**54.5km**).

TERMIGNON

The attractive village of Termignon, on the southern edge of the Vanoise national park, has a smattering of shops and restaurants while Maison de la Vanoise has a permanent exhibition offering a view of life in the Vanoise through the seasons. Other attractions of note in the village include the pink-painted Notre-Dame-de-la-Visitation chapel – built in 1536 and first named Notre-Dame-du-Poivre due to its position on the spice route from Lyon to Milan – and the sombre Luc Jaggi-Couvert sculpted war memorial which remembers the fallen of World War 1. The statue depicts a grieving woman dressed in traditional costume mourning the loss of a loved one, her right hand raised to her face.

STAGE 7
Val Cenis Termignon to Valloire

Start	Maison de la Vanoise, Val Cenis Termignon (1299m)
Finish	Tourist office, Valloire (1406m)
Distance	51.5km (32 miles)
Total ascent	940m
Total descent	833m
Maximum elevation	1581m
Major passes	Col du Télégraphe (1566m)
Refreshments	Modane (17km), St-Michel-de-Maurienne (34km), Col du Télégraphe (46.5km)

Stage 7 continues to follow the route of the Arc, the sounds of rushing white water ever present when the river is in full flow. The stage skirts the southern border of the Vanoise national park and continues through the Maurienne valley to the busy town of Modane, passing the formidable Forts de l'Esseillon. From Modane the road continues to descend, the busy A43 Autoroute and railway line now rarely far away, to Saint-Michel-de-Maurienne. Wave goodbye to the Arc as a left-hand turn in town crosses the river for the start of the Col du Télégraphe. After 12km of ascent a welcome 5km drop into Valloire completes the stage.

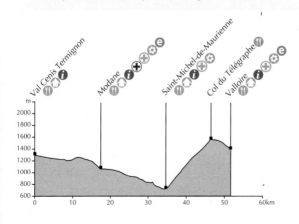

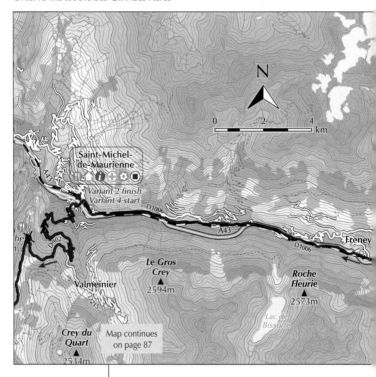

Map continues
on page 87

Rising below the Ancien Glacier des Trois Becs and the Glacier des Sources de l'Arc, the Arc flows for nearly 128km through the Maurienne valley before meeting the Isère.

With the Maison de la Vanoise on your left, proceed on the D1006, crossing a bridge and passing the small but arresting war monument. The road drops out of Termignon as it follows the path of the river Arc. ◄

After passing through Sollières-Sardières, Le Verney and the outskirts of **Bramans**, the road nears the impressive Forts de l'Esseillon, which will appear on your right (**11.6km**).

Built in the early 19th century, the **Forts de l'Esseillon** comprise five fortified buildings placed to guard passage from France in the west through the valley to Mont Cenis. With perpendicular

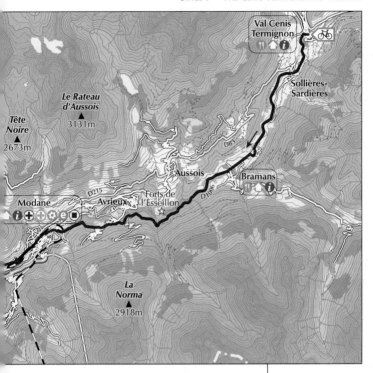

fortifications and cannon towers, they were constructed to protect the Kingdom of Piedmont-
Sardinia from French invasion. Each of the forts
is named after a member of the House of Savoy:
the Marie-Thérèse redoubt, Fort Victor-Emmanuel,
Fort Charles-Félix, Fort Marie-Christine and Fort
Charles-Albert. The four forts stand on the northern bank of the Arc river, with the redoubt on the
south. A small bridge dubbed the Pont du Diable
(Devil's Bridge) links them. Three of the forts have
been renovated and declared historic monuments.
Today, a number of walking routes allow you to
explore the site.

The Frejus rail tunnel links Modane with Bardonecchia in Italy. Opened in 1871 and initially 12.8km long, the tunnel, at that time, was the longest in the world.

After passing the forts, the road immediately crosses a bridge over a splendid gorge with the wide road twisting and turning as the descent to Modane continues, the town soon coming into view. ◄

After entering **Modane** (**16.9km**) continue to the roundabout with a small stone bridge in the middle and take the second exit (SP: D1006/A43/Saint-Michel-de-Maurienne). At the next roundabout continue straight on.

Continue on the D1006 to exit Modane and immediately enter Fourneaux (**19.5km**). At the next roundabout continue straight on (SP: D1006/A43/Saint-Michel-de-Maurienne) to leave the bustle of Modane and Fourneaux behind. Remain on the D1006 to Saint-Michel-de-Maurienne.   The 120km-long Maurienne valley runs south-west from Ecot to Modane and then west/north-west to Aiton. Many famous climbs rise from the valley, with it dubbed the 'world's largest cycling area'.

The imposing Esseillon forts were built between 1815 and 1830

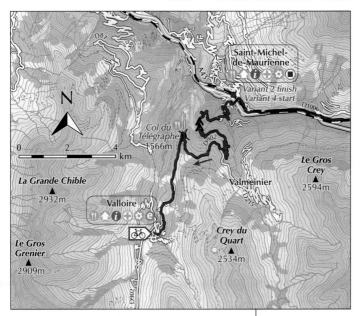

After entering **Saint-Michel-de-Maurienne** go under a railway bridge and pass the fire station on your left. At the traffic lights (**34.4km**) turn left (SP: D902/Valloire/Col du Télégraphe) and take the bridge over the river to start the Col du Télégraphe. ▶

From Saint-Michel-de-Maurienne the Col du Télégraphe is 11.9km long at an average of 7%.

In 1911, when the Alps were introduced to the route of the Tour de France, Émile Georget was the first to lead the race over the **Col du Télégraphe**, although he is more celebrated for leading the way over the Col du Galibier a few hours later. Indeed, if the Télégraphe was positioned anywhere else it would rightly be regarded as a serious climb in its own right. As it is, the climb is often regarded merely as the support act for the Galibier, its more intimidating neighbour. As the main summer route between the Maurienne valley to the north and the

87

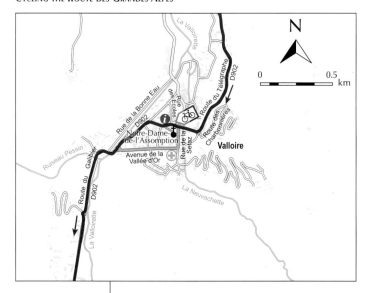

Guisane and Romanche valleys to the south, it can be busy with traffic, but the road is pleasant and climbs through an agreeable wood. Where the trees thin, you can glimpse pleasing views north over the Maurienne valley.

Remain on the D902 as it weaves its way up the mountain in a series of hairpins to the summit of the **Col du Télégraphe**, where there is a café and, usually, a giant sculpture of something made from straw (**46.5km**).

From the top of the pass descend to **Valloire**. At the first roundabout in Valloire take the first exit (SP: Col du Galibier). The tourist office and the end point of the stage will be on your right, opposite the Notre-Dame-de-l'Assomption church (**51.4km**)

VALLOIRE

A straw sculpture at the top of the Col du Télégraphe

The gateway to the Galibier, Valloire has long been a magnet for visitors who are attracted by the remarkable setting of what remains a relatively remote town. The first tourists arrived in the 1850s and by 1914 the town claimed a grand total of 50 beds in 4 hotels. Today that number is reported to be over 17,500 beds across more than 2000 properties built to service those who come every winter to enjoy the 150km of pistes accessible from the town. In summer hundreds of cyclists flock to the town daily, all aiming to scale the famous Galibier.

Beyond being a winter and summer sporting playground, Valloire offers some culture in the form of a number of small chapels that dot the valley from the top of the Télégraphe to the hamlet of Bonnenuit on the Galibier road, although these can only be viewed from outside. The remarkable Notre-Dame-de-l'Assomption church, consecrated in 1682, stands in the middle of town. If open, it is well worth a visit to admire the baroque art and frescoes that decorate the interior of the church.

The town is also home to a number of international sculpture competitions: in winter pieces formed from snow and ice abound while in summer teams are provided with 600kg of hay, 400kg of straw, wooden rafters, twisted irons, wire, nails and mesh with which to construct their masterpieces.

STAGE 8
Valloire to Briançon

Start	Tourist office, Valloire (1406m)
Finish	Rond-Point des Alpes, Briançon (1259m)
Distance	52.75km (32¾ miles)
Total ascent	1235m
Total descent	1382m
Maximum elevation	2642m
Major passes	Col du Galibier (2642m)
Refreshments	Plan Lachat (9.8km), Les Granges (13.6km), Tunnel du Galibier (17km), Col du Lautaret (26.6km), Le Monêtier-les-Bains (39.4km), La Salle-les-Alpes (44.5km)

The main course on the menu that is Stage 8 is the Col du Galibier, literally one of the high points of the entire route. Peaking at over 2640m, this barren but dramatic pass is a mammoth undertaking and the scene of countless famous exploits undertaken by the stars of the Tour de France. It is a tough but rewarding ride, a climb to be respected amid the towering summits of the Massif des Cerces. At the top of the pass, the route crosses from the Savoie into the Hautes-Alpes department. There follows a sharp drop to the Col du Lautaret and then a long and sweeping descent, passing the 45th parallel, through the villages of the Serre Chevalier ski resort, before arriving in the stunning town of Briançon.

With Valloire's tourist office on your right proceed over the small, paved section of road on Rue des Grandes Alpes. Follow the road round to the left to a small round-about. Proceed straight on and cross a small bridge over the Valloirette river. Pass a chapel on your right before crossing another small bridge. At the next roundabout take the second exit to remain on the D902 and start the climb of the Col du Galibier. ◄

From the tourist office in Valloire the Col du Galibier is 18.2km at an average of 6.8%.

It is a long, straight and sometimes steep drag out of Valloire, passing ski lifts and *télécabines* (gondolas). It

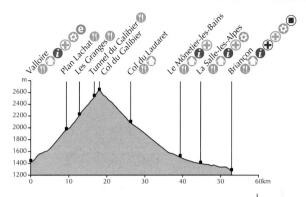

isn't until exiting **Les Verneys** (**3km**) that you finally leave the buildings of the resort behind.

Follow the D902 to the summit of the Galibier. This climb is one of the route's toughest tests: it's high, it's long and it's steep. It is also a climb of two distinct sections. The first 10km or so follows the path of the Valloirette river. Always climbing, the terrain grows starker as you gain height, the road cutting through scree slopes with the high peaks of the Massif des Cerces guarding the road. After you have passed the auberge at **Plan Lachat** (**9.8km**), the second section of the climb begins as the road hairpins to the right and crosses the Valloirette before steepening markedly. From here it is a relentless grind to the top, the gradient rarely dipping below 8% as the road twists and turns up the mountain passing the hamlet of **Les Granges**.

> Among the tiny collection of buildings that comprises **Les Granges** (**13.5km**) is La Ferme du Galibier, which, if open, offers the opportunity to purchase some local produce, including cheese and meats, and stocks a small selection of refreshments. Next to the farm shop is a small monument to the Italian rider Marco Pantani. It was here that Pantani made a move that would ultimately deliver him the 1998 Tour de France. In terrible weather

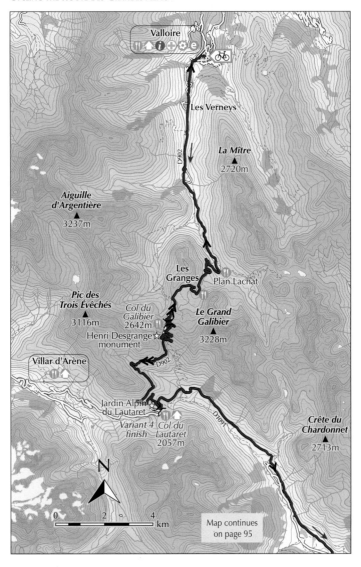

Valloire

Les Verneys

La Mître
▲
2720m

Aiguille
d'Argentière
▲
3237m

Les
Granges

Plan Lachat

Pic des
Trois Évêchés
▲
3116m

Col du
Galibier
2642m

Le Grand
Galibier
▲
3228m

Henri Desgrange
monument

Villar d'Arène

Jardin Alpin
du Lautaret

Variant 4
finish

Col du
Lautaret
2057m

Crête du
Chardonnet
▲
2713m

N

0   2   4 km

Map continues
on page 95

he attacked the group of favourites he was with, exploding up the road like a rocket. He crested the Galibier with a two-minute advantage and won the stage in Les Deux Alpes by nearly six minutes to claim the yellow jersey.

The Galibier is not a particularly attractive climb. High above the treeline, it is exposed, harsh and desolate; impressive and grandiose rather than pretty. At the car tunnel entrance take the road to the left (D902B) for the final 1.5km haul to the top – bikes are forbidden to use the tunnel. After pausing at the summit of the **Col du Galibier** to enjoy the remarkable views – south, to the 4102m Barre des Écrins and out over the Serre Chevalier valley to the west – continue by passing into the Hautes-Alpes department for a technical descent to the Col du Lautaret, taking care at the traffic lights that control the flow of traffic at the southern side of the tunnel.

Standing on the southern flank of the Galibier is a monument dedicated to **Henri Desgrange**, the

Posing for the obligatory snapshot at the top of the Galibier

The Guisane valley is an enjoyable descent, from the Col du Lautaret to Briançon

father of the Tour de France. Desgrange introduced the high Alps into the race route in 1911 and was particularly struck by the Galibier. With the majority of riders forced to walk, Desgrange, no stranger to employing hyperbolic prose in his reporting, was moved to write: 'Oh Sappey, oh Laffrey, oh Col Bayard, oh Tourmalet! I shall not fail in my duty to proclaim to the world that you are like pale and common wine compared to the Galibier: all one can do before this giant is doff one's hat and bow.'

Just before the junction a right-hand turn onto a gravelled path takes you to the Jardin Alpin du Lautaret, which displays more than 2000 species of mountain flora.

At the junction with the **Col du Lautaret** (**26.6km**) turn left (SP: D1091/Briançon). ◄

Follow the long and sweeping descent through avalanche tunnels towards the villages of the Serre Chevalier valley. This road is the main route between Grenoble and Briançon and so is rarely anything but busy. But the descent is an enjoyable one as the road follows the path of the Guisane river.

Always remaining on the D1091, pass through the resorts of **Le Monêtier-les-Bains** (**39.4km**),

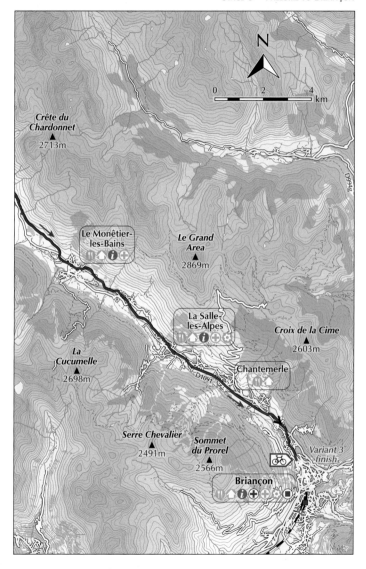

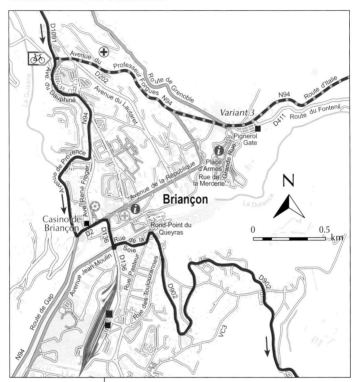

La Salle-les-Alpes (**44.5km**) and **Chantemerle** (**47.5km**), until you arrive at a roundabout with a large gondola in the middle (**50.3km**). Take the second exit (SP: D1091/ Briançon) to enter **Briançon** (**51km**). Descend through the outskirts of the town to reach the Rond-Point des Alpes and the finish of the stage. This is also the end point of Variant 3 (**52.7km**).

BRIANÇON

The attractive and fortified old town of Briançon is ripe for exploration

At the foot of three high mountain passes – the Col de Montgenèvre, Col d'Izoard and Col de Lautaret – and the intersection of five valleys, the fortified town of Briançon has long held an important strategic position. While visitors come to explore the Écrins national park and the towns and villages that combine to form the resort of Serre Chevalier, Briançon is far more than just an entrance point into the natural splendours that surround the town.

Perched at 1326m on a rocky outcrop high above modern Briançon is the UNESCO-protected citadel. Fortifications have existed here since Roman times and have undergone various reconstructions and reinforcements over the subsequent centuries. However, in 1692 Vauban, a military engineer, criticised the developments and recommended a series of improvements. While his plans were never fully realised, old Briançon is today synonymous with the military engineer who can claim the fortification of some 300 locations.

A few days can easily be spent here exploring the old town and its surroundings. Attractions include the narrow Rue de la Mercerie with its ochre-coloured facades, the Pignerol Gate, the Place d'Armes and the interesting shops and cafés that line the cobbled Grand Rue. Further afield are the Salettes Fort to the north-east and the single-span Asfeld bridge, which crosses the Durance river, just outside the eastern walls.

STAGE 9
Briançon to Guillestre

Start	Rond-Point des Alpes, Briançon (1259m)
Finish	Rond-Point Le Château, Guillestre (1039m)
Distance	52.25km (32½ miles)
Total ascent	1575m
Total descent	1795m
Maximum elevation	2363m
Major passes	Col d'Izoard (2360m)
Refreshments	Cervières (11.5km), Le Laus (13.7km) Refuge Napoléon – Izoard (20.5km) Le Brunissard (28.6km) Arvieux (31.7km)

From historic Briançon, the route heads into the southern Alps as Stage 9 passes over the immense Col d'Izoard, where a monument commemorates the work of the builders of the RdGA. The subsequent descent through the rocky moonscape of the Casse Déserte is nothing short of breathtaking. After a short climb there follows a wonderful descent through the Queyras regional park, the narrow road cutting through rock faces and bordering the river Guil as you head to the finish on the outskirts of Guillestre.

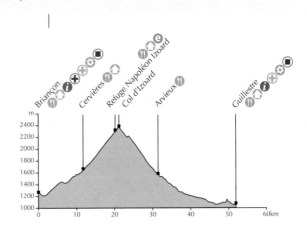

98

From the Rond-Point des Alpes in Briançon, take the exit signposted Gap/Sisteron/Col d'Izoard onto Avenue du Dauphiné. Follow signs for Gare SNCF and continue straight on to Avenue de Provence. Cross a bridge over the Guisane and pass the Prorel gondola. At the traffic lights turn left (SP: Col d'Izoard/Centre Ville). Pass the Casino de Briançon on the left and at the next roundabout take the first exit (SP: Col d'Izoard). Pass over the Durance and at the roundabout take the third exit onto Rue de la Soie (SP: Col d'Izoard). Continue to a T-junction and turn left onto Rue Pasteur. At the Rond-Point du Queyras take the first exit (SP: Col d'Izoard/Parc Regional du Queyras) to finally leave the maze of busy roads behind and start the climb of the Col d'Izoard. ▸

The well-paved D902 now rises, offering views over the town and the valley beyond. The climb starts in earnest after exiting the village of **Cervières** (**11.2km**), the road rising steeply after a right-hand hairpin. There is an increasing feeling of exposure as the road rises through the pine forest via more hairpins before emerging above

The view north from the Col d'Izoard with Refuge Napoléon below

From Briançon the Col d'Izoard is 20km at an average of 5.7%.

99

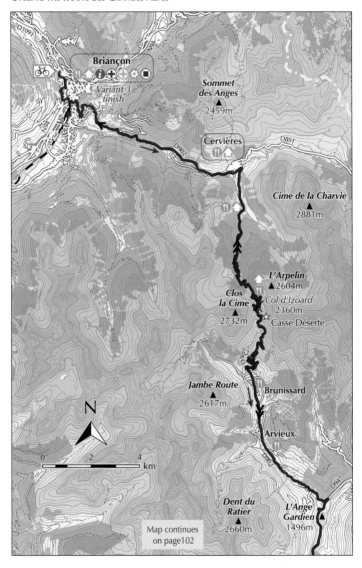

Briançon

Variant 3 finish

Sommet des Anges
▲ 2459m

Cervières

Cime de la Charvie
▲ 2881m

L'Arpelin
▲ 2604m

Col d'Izoard
2360m

Clos la Cime
▲ 2732m

Casse Déserte

Jambe Route
▲ 2617m

Brunissard

Arvieux

N

0   2   4
km

Dent du Ratier
▲ 2660m

L'Ange Gardien
▲ 1496m

Map continues on page102

the treeline and passing the Refuge Napoléon (**20.5km**). The top of the pass comes 1km further on. ▶

Standing at the top of the Col d'Izoard is a **monument** to those who built the road over the mountain in 1897. Erected in 1934 by the Touring Club of France, and built from stone, the monument commemorates the work of General Baron Berge and the Alpine troops who constructed the high and strategic passes of the Izoard, Vars and Cayolle, which later enabled the realisation of the Route des Alpes project.

From the top of the **Col d'Izoard** the road descends through the remarkable **Casse Déserte**, passing a couple of small monuments on the right dedicated to the professional cyclists Fausto Coppi and Louison Bobet. ▶

Classified as a natural monument in 1937, the **Casse Déserte** is one of the most remarkable landscapes through which the RdGA passes. The rock here is a mix of dolomite and limestone, and their

The Izoard's Refuge Napoléon was one of six Alpine refuges built under Napoleon III to shelter travellers 'surprised by storms or stopped by avalanches'. It was completed in 1858.

Coppi and Bobet are two legendary riders with five Tour de France wins between them. Both became synonymous with the Izoard, Coppi leading the race over the summit twice, Bobet three times.

The remarkable Casse Déserte comes a couple of kilometres into the descent of the Izoard

varying properties mean they erode differently thus forming *cargneules*: the monoliths of serrated stone that tower over the road. It makes for a unique environment. Often referred to as lunar-like there is also an air of the Wild West about it. It is well worth a little time off the bike here to fully immerse yourself in this special place.

After a stiff climb out of the Casse Déserte, the road descends through tight hairpins before emerging

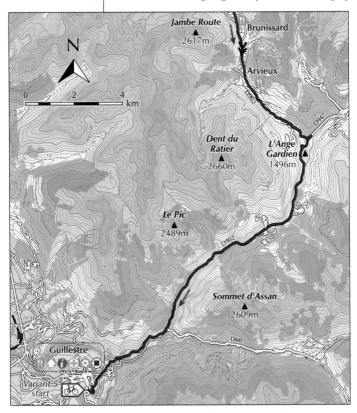

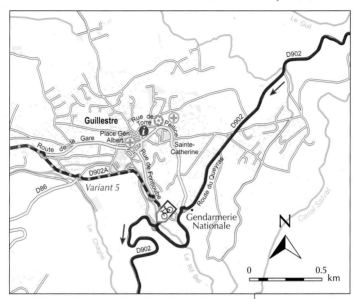

onto a high Alpine plain just before the community of
Brunissard (**28.6km**). From here the road straightens for
the next 7km. At the junction with the D947 (**35.7km**)
turn right (SP: Guillestre) to remain on the D902. The
route now descends through the picturesque Queyras
regional park, the narrow road cutting through a spectacular gorge and picking up the Guil river.

> The highest peak in the **Queyras regional park** is
> Pic Nord de la Font Sancte, which stands at 3385m,
> although it is dominated by Italy's Monte Viso, the
> highest mountain in the Cottian Alps and against
> which the south-east of the region borders. It is on
> these slopes that the Guil river rises before wind-
> ing its way through the park and flowing into the
> Durance at Guillestre.

Remain on the D902, taking care through a number of dark tunnels that have been hacked through the rock, at length entering **Guillestre** (**50.8km**). At the first roundabout – Porte du Queyras (also the start point of Variant 5) – take the second exit (SP: Vars/Risoul). The road passes through trees as it curves right to a second roundabout and the end of the stage – Rond-Point Le Château (**52.2km**).

GUILLESTRE

Gateway to the Queyras and at the foot of the passes of the Izoard, Vars and Agnel, Guillestre sits at the confluence of the Guil and Durance valleys.

The attractive old town is surrounded by the remains of protective medieval walls as well as a series of entrance gates named after saints and adorned with effigies. Pastel houses nestle in narrow streets, while the Place Albert is the centre of Guillestre's café culture. The town's Notre-Dame d'Aquilon church was consecrated in 1532, and its pillared porch includes a pair of sculpted lions supporting the columns, while its three-storey square bell tower features a sundial.

Some 5km north-west of Guillestre is the Forte de Mont-Dauphin. Completed in 1700, the fortress was designed by Vauban on the orders of King Louis XIV after the Duke of Savoy's army crossed the Vars and invaded Guillestre, Embrun and Gap in 1692. The Duke's army was ultimately forced to retreat due to disease and poor weather but the invasion highlighted the vulnerability of the area. The plateau on which the fortress was built, at a strategic crossroads of valleys that guarded the access to the Dauphiné and Provence, was named 'the thousand winds'.

Impressive as the fort was and remains, Vauban's plans were never fully realised. Its importance was diminished once France gave up Piedmont to Savoy for Ubaye in 1713. At its peak Mont-Dauphin counted 1000 soldiers and 400 civilians as inhabitants, some 600 shy of Vauban's planned population.

STAGE 10

Guillestre to Barcelonnette

Start	Rond-Point Le Château, Guillestre (1039m)
Finish	Place Aimé Gassier, Barcelonnette (1140m)
Distance	49.25km (30½ miles)
Total ascent	1170m
Total descent	1069m
Maximum elevation	2114m
Major passes	Col de Vars (2108m)
Refreshments	Vars Les Claux (13.1km), Refuge Napoléon – Vars (16.6km), Col de Vars (18.9km), La Condamine (35.2km), Jausiers (40km)

Stage 10 leaves the Queyras bound for the Ubaye valley via the 2109m Col de Vars, the road climbing through the various resorts of the functional ski station of Vars before reaching the top of the pass and crossing into the Alpes-de-Haute-Provence department. A steep and enjoyable descent on good roads follows, skirting the small but diverting village of Saint-Paul-sur-Ubaye, heading for the Mexican villas of Jausiers. The end of the stage is in the centre of attractive Barcelonnette, a flat 9km further along the valley.

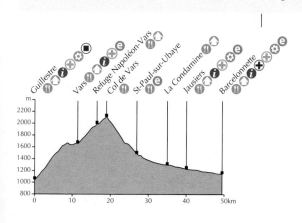

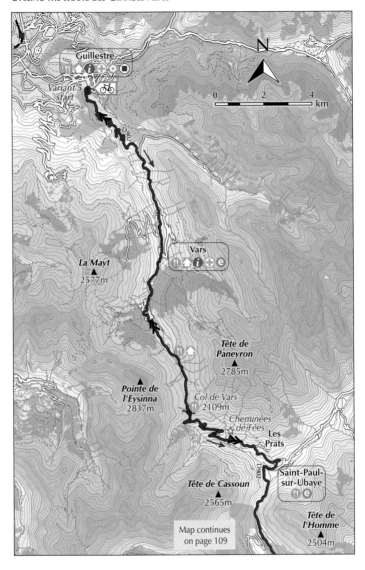

Guillestre

Variant 5 start

La Mayt
2577m

Vars

Pointe de l'Eysinna
2837m

Tête de Paneyron
2785m

Col de Vars
2109m

Cheminées de Fées

Les Prats

Tête de Cassoun
2565m

Saint-Paul-sur-Ubaye

Tête de l'Homme
2504m

Map continues on page 109

The climb of the Col de Vars affords glorious views north over the Écrins

At the Rond-Point Le Château, on the southern outskirts of Guillestre and the end point of the previous stage, take the exit signposted D902/Vars. ▶

The first 8km or so of the climb is difficult, with long sections of an 8% gradient or more as the road twists up the mountain. Eventually, the road flattens, even falling for 1km or so, as the pistes of the **Vars** ski station, carved out of the larch-clad mountainside, come into view. After exiting Vars Sainte-Marie, the road tips skywards again as you continue traversing the villages of the ski resort.

From Guillestre the Col de Vars is 19km at an average of 5.7km.

Combining the villages of Saint-Marcellin, Saint-Catherine, Sainte-Marie and Les Claux, modern-day **Vars** is a sprawling resort that starts some 10km below the summit of the pass and stretches for 5km along the D902. Saint-Marcellin is the oldest of the villages and objects dating from the Bronze Age have been found here. The resort's first ski infra-structure was built in Saint-Marie in the 1930s. Today, a 3.6km walking route invites you to 'find the treasures' of the villages, which include sundials, fountains and wooden sculptures.

Bicycles aren't the only way to ride to the top of the Col de Vars

The Alpes-de-Haute-Provence department was known as the Basses-Alpes until 1970. Created in 1790 during the French Revolution, it was home to some 164,000 people in 2017 according to the census.

Remain on the D902, climbing through Vars Les Claux (**13.1km**) to emerge onto a high plateau. Pass the Refuge Napoléon (**16.6km**), which stands opposite a large pond. Despite the altitude now approaching 2000m, the environment is very different to that of the Izoard, with grass and water surrounding you as opposed to rock and scree.

An exposed 2km haul to the summit of the **Col de Vars** follows (**18.9km**), which marks the point of entry into the Alpes-de-Haute-Provence department. ◄

Follow the D902 for a steep descent with sweeping bends. Take care to look out for the Cheminées de Fées, a cluster of 'fairy chimneys' formed by erosion, which will appear on your left after you have exited the tiny community of Mélèzen and crossed a bridge over the Torrent du Peinier (**23.8km**).

Pass a turning to **Saint-Paul-sur-Ubaye** (**27.2km**) and pick up the path of the Ubaye river. At length exit Les Gleizolles (**33.4km**). At the following junction turn right (SP: D900/Gap/Barcelonnette) and cross the Ubayette river.

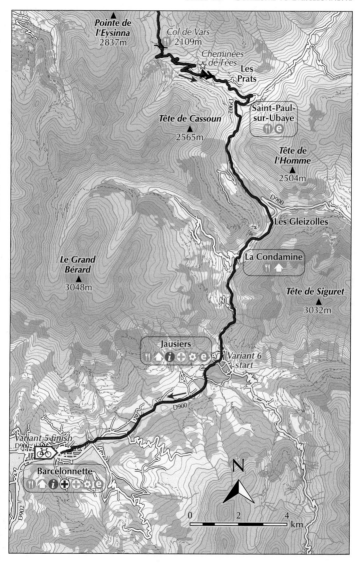

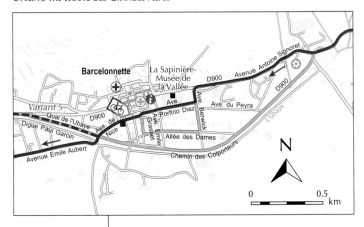

The tiny community of **Saint-Paul-sur-Ubaye** is worth pausing your descent for a wander. Among the interesting buildings, many of which have corrugated roofs, is a museum dedicated to Albert Manuel, the village's former blacksmith. The museum tells the story of past agricultural work, transport and forgotten trades. Some 4.5km north-east of the town, along the D25, is the Pont du Châtelet. Completed in 1882, the bridge joins two sheer cliff faces. At 108m high and with an 18m span it is claimed to have the second greatest height-to-span ratio in the world.

Jausiers is the start point of Variant 6, which takes in the formidable 2715m-high Col de Bonette.

Barcelonnette is also the finish point of Variant 5.

Proceed on the D900, skirting the Ubaye river into **Jausiers** (40km). ◄

Pass through the town, remaining on the D900, and continue to **Barcelonnette** (**47.6km**). After passing the junction with the D209, proceed along Avenue Antoine Signoret, passing grand villas before following the road round to the left. Turn right onto Avenue Porfirio Diaz (SP: Toutes Directions), passing Parc de la Sapinière, and continue straight on to emerge onto Place Aimé Gassier and the end point of the stage (**49.2km**). ◄

110

BARCELONNETTE

The narrow streets of Barcelonnette

Nestled in the heart of the Ubaye valley, the handsome town of Barcelonnette dates from the 13th century. Despite its altitude of 1135m, the feeling here is not one of a mountain community but of a once-important town of wealth.

Barcelonnette's myriad of streets and pleasing squares make for an interesting morning's stroll. The town is famous for its impressive, if unexpected, grand villas that line the streets on the outskirts of town.

The heritage of these villas lies thousands of miles away over the Atlantic. First, Jacques Arnaud left the Ubaye valley in the early 1800s, settling in Louisiana with his two brothers and paving the way for others to follow his path to the Americas. And follow they did. The people of the Ubaye valley had long worked in textiles, and in the 1820s they took their trade over the Atlantic, to Mexico, with great success.

It is claimed that by the end of the 1800s the Ubaye valley accounted for some 70% of Mexican textile trading. When the exiles returned home to Ubaye, many used their wealth to build the splendid villas seen around the town today. Over the course of 50 years some 80 such examples were built in and around Barcelonnette and Jausiers. The only villa open to the public is La Sapinière; built in 1878, it is where the Musée de la Vallée can be found.

Barcelonnette celebrates its link with Mexico with an annual, week-long festival dubbed the Fêtes Latino-Mexicaines, usually held in August.

STAGE 11
Barcelonnette to Valberg

Start	Place Aimé Gassier, Barcelonnette (1140m)
Finish	Avenue de Valberg, Valberg (1678m)
Distance	75.25km (46¾ miles)
Total ascent	2400m
Total descent	1862m
Maximum elevation	2329m
Major passes	Col de la Cayolle (2326m); Col de Valberg (1672m)
Refreshments	Refuge Hotel de Bayasse (20.4km), Refuge de la Cayolle (28.7km), Refuge de la Cantonnière (35.8km), Entraunes (44.1km), Guillaumes (61.2km)

Tough but rewarding, Stage 11 introduces the wild and spectacular Mercantour National Park. From Barcelonnette the route heads over the captivating Col de la Cayolle, perhaps the most delightful ascent of the entire RdGA, following the Bachelard river and passing through green gorges and criss-crossing old bridges. From the top of the Cayolle there is a long and steep descent alongside the river Var to the sun-drenched town of Guillaumes. A stiff 12km climb to the serviceable ski town of Valberg completes the stage.

Starting in Barcelonnette's Place Aimé Gassier, with Restaurant Les Copains behind you and the gravelled square used by locals for pétanque to your left, proceed straight ahead, passing a bus stop on your left. Follow signs for the Col de la Cayolle and proceed along Avenue de Nice. Cross the Pont du Plan over the Ubaye and follow the road around to the right to proceed along Avenue Émile Aubert (SP: D902/Col de la Cayolle).

Shortly after exiting Barcelonnette (**2.6km**), the road splits. Take the left-hand turning (SP: D902/Uvernet-Fours/Col de la Cayolle). Note: the right-hand option (SP: D908/Pra-Loup) offers an alternative and tougher

route that passes over the Col d'Allos and the Col des Champs. This option is narrow and steep in places so care is needed. For the Allos alternative follow the D908 to Colmars, then immediately take the narrow left-hand turning to the Col des Champs. Descend on the D78 to rejoin the route at St-Martin-d'Entraunes (67.6km/2010m).

The Col de la Cayolle is one of the highlights of the entire route

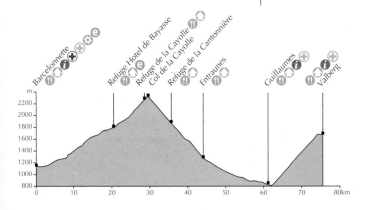

Cyclist scanning the mountainside for marmots at the Col de la Cayolle

Follow the D902 through **Uvernet-Fours**, traversing the Gorges du Bachelard, and passing the Refuges of Bayasse and the Cayolle, before reaching the top of the **Col de la Cayolle (29.6km)**.

With an average gradient of just over 4%, the **Col de la Cayolle** is perhaps the most pleasing of all the Alpine passes used by the RdGA. At 2326m it is the final climb of the route that breaks 2000m in altitude but for the most part does not feel like a high Alpine pass. The narrow road strikes through a spectacular gorge before a right-hand hairpin at Bayasse crosses a tight bridge. The road then steepens, with the final 5km to the exposed pass the toughest part of the climb. Often-shy marmots can sometimes be seen during what is a truly spectacular ride.

The top of the Col de la Cayolle is the border between the Alpes-de-Haute-Provence and the Alpes-Maritimes departments and the road changes number from D902 to D2202. The descent from the top of the Cayolle is steep and technical, the narrow road falling

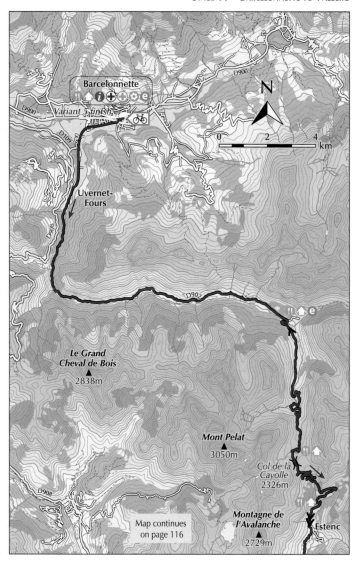

Map continues
on page 116

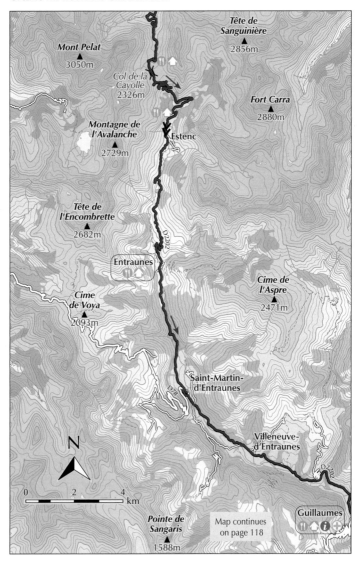

Mont Pelat
3050m

Tête de
Sanguinière
2856m

Col de la
Cayolle
2326m

Fort Carra
2880m

Montagne de
l'Avalanche
2729m

Estenc

Tête de
l'Encombrette
2682m

D2202

Entraunes

Cime de
l'Aspre
2471m

Cime
de Voya
2093m

Saint-Martin-
d'Entraunes

D78

Villeneuve-
d'Entraunes

D2202

Guillaumes

N

0   2   4
km

Pointe de
Sangaris
1588m

Map continues
on page 118

Sunbaked Guillaumes offers a chance for refreshment

down the mountain in a series of tight bends. While the views beyond over the Mercantour are diverting, and the folded layers of rock surrounding you form interesting and almost face-like patterns, close attention needs to be paid to the road in front of you, with dark tunnels that also need to be navigated. After 7km or so of descent, just before the hamlet of Estenc, is the source of the Var. ▸

The river Var flows for 114km, broadly south-east, through the Alpes-Maritimes before flowing into the Mediterranean by Nice airport.

After passing through a strikingly barren field of black rock, traverse **Entraunes (44.2km)** and **St-Martin-d'Entraunes (49.9km)** – where the Col d'Allos/Col des Champs option returns to the main route. The long descent off the Cayolle finally ends in the town of **Guillaumes (61.4km)**, a small and pleasant community with an interesting old town complete with religious murals and houses adorned with brightly painted decorative plaques. ▸

Some 7.5km off-route to the south of Guillaumes lies the Gorges de Daluis, a canyon of 6km that has been dubbed the 'Colorado Niçois.' because of its distinctive red hue.

Traverse Guillaumes and its cafés and restaurants. Pass the town's pharmacy and a fountain on your right and then, immediately after crossing a bridge, turn left (SP: D28/Valberg) to finally leave the D2202 and start the climb to Valberg. From Guillaumes the Col de Valberg is 12.2km at an average of 6%.

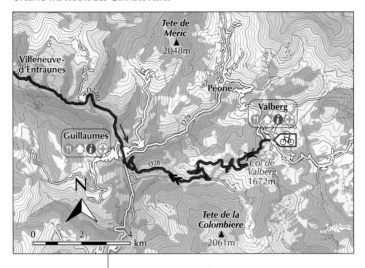

Opposite the fountain in Guillaumes is a turning for the **D29**. This alternative option wriggles upwards from Guillaumes for just over 14km before reaching Valberg. It is narrower and longer than the main route but offers the opportunity to visit the village of Péone. Nestled under a distinctive collection of Dolomitic pillars, this medieval village is a delightful warren of narrow streets ripe for exploring. The village claims to be the birthplace of not one but two queens, both born in the 1770s: Marie Julie Clary, who became the Queen of Naples and Spain, and Désirée Clary, who became the Queen of Sweden and Norway.

Follow the D28 for nearly 13km as it twists upwards towards Valberg, a difficult climax to a long and testing stage. Pass the Col de Valberg sign (**74km**) and continue into **Valberg** itself. At the first roundabout (Note: the D29/Péone alternative route also enters town here.) dismount to traverse the pedestrianised Avenue de Valberg where the stage finishes (**75.3km**).

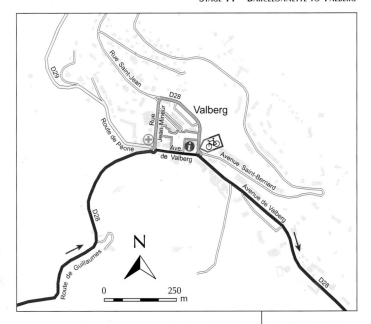

THE MERCANTOUR NATIONAL PARK

Valberg is centrally situated in the Mercantour, a wild and bewitching national park where wolves roam and true wilderness never seems far away.

The park is defined by two massifs – limestone in the north-west, crystalline in the south-east – split by the Tinée river. Comprising six valleys and the departments of the Alpes-Maritimes and Alpes-de-Haute-Provence, the Mercantour is the final sweep of the southern Alps before they plunge into the Mediterranean. Indeed, the highest peak, the 3143m Cime du Gélas, stands on the French/Italian border just 50km from the sea as the crow flies.

The park is characterised by forests and valleys, gorges and white-water torrents and hair-raising roads. There are glacial lakes to explore, including the Lac d'Allos, the largest natural glacier lake in Europe, which sits at an altitude of 2220m, as well as the 3000m+ peaks. It all adds up to a place of real adventure and it can be no surprise that the Mercantour has been described as 'nature on steroids'.

STAGE 12
Valberg to Saint-Martin-Vésubie

Start	Avenue de Valberg, Valberg (1678m)
Finish	Place du Général de Gaulle, Saint-Martin-Vésubie (970m)
Distance	58.75km (36½ miles)
Total ascent	1585m
Total descent	2293m
Maximum elevation	1678m
Major passes	Col de la Couillole (1678m); Col Saint Martin (1500m)
Refreshments	Beuil (6km), Roubion (18.3km) Saint-Sauveur-sur-Tinée (29.7km), Valdeblore-La Bolline (42.1km), Valdeblore-Saint-Dalmas (47.1km)

A 58km ride east through the Mercantour National Park, Stage 12 takes in three passes – although with some 540km and 12 mountain passes over 11 stages now already in the legs, the first two will barely register. After the Col de Ste-Anne and Col de la Couillole there follows a precipitous and narrow descent to Saint-Sauveur-sur-Tinée. A ride through the Tinée valley is followed by a long and difficult ascent to the Col Saint Martin. A 10km descent to the pleasing town of Saint-Martin-Vésubie completes the stage.

At the eastern end of Valberg's pedestrianised Avenue de Valberg, and with Bar le Sapet on your left, take the road in front of you which goes to the right (SP: Beuil/Nice). Continue straight over the next roundabout to remain on the D28 and exit Valberg (**1.4km**).

Follow the D28 as it descends to Beuil via the Col de Ste-Anne. Shortly after entering **Beuil (5.8km)**, take the left-hand turning by the Relais du Mercantour bar and service station (SP: D30/Saint-Sauveur-sur-Tinée/Roubion). The D30 continues to descend for half a kilometre before starting to climb the Col de la Couillole. ◀

The Col de la Couillole is 7.2km at an average of 3.2%.

Continue to the top of the **Col de la Couillole** (**13.4km**), where the road becomes the M30, before starting a dramatic and precipitous 16km downhill ride. This is a steep, narrow and winding descent, with the mountainside falling steeply away from the road, passing waterfalls and riding through tunnels. While extra

The heavily wooded slopes of the descent of the Col de la Couillole

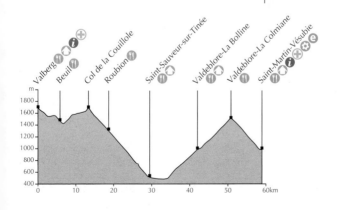

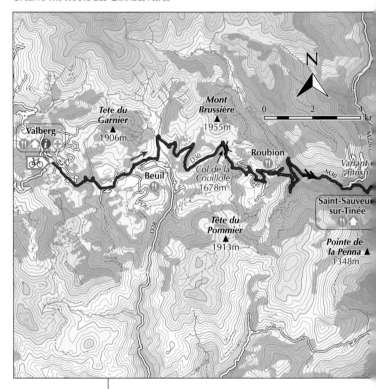

Ubiquitous broom bushes border the road, almost lighting the way. The yellow flowers of this fragrant plant were once used in the making of beer before the introduction of hops.

care is undoubtedly needed here, be sure to take time to stop and enjoy the far-reaching views over the steep gorges and the Tinée valley below. They are nothing short of stunning. ◄

Around 5km into the descent from the Col de la Couillole is a left-hand turn that leads to **Roubion**. Described by its tourism website as 'hanging on the cliff like an eagle's nest', the village comprises old and attractive houses surrounded by ramparts, built in the 12th century, from which magnificent views can be enjoyed. With just 120 permanent residents

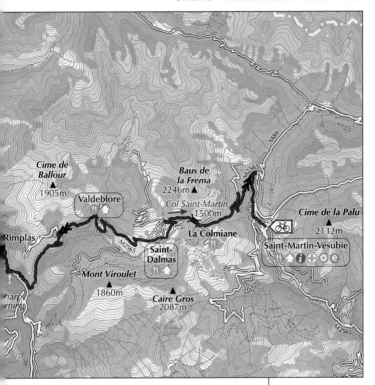

at the last census, Roubion has several buildings of interest, including the 16th-century Chapelle Saint-Sébastien with its splendid murals. Meanwhile the artist Imelda Bassanello has painted a number of doors in the village in celebration of the community's past.

At length the M30 reaches a junction with the M2205 (the end point of Variant 6). Turn right (SP: M2205/Saint-Sauveur-sur-Tinée/Nice) and traverse the small town of **Saint-Sauveur-sur-Tinée** (**30km**) as the road picks up the path of the Tinée river. ▶

The Tinée rises near the Col de la Bonette and flows for 70km before meeting the Var some 6km north of Bonson.

Proceed on the M2205, with sheer rock and high wooded slopes on your left and the Tinée river below and to your right. After a long left-hand bend, and just before a tunnel, pull over by the Rimplas Gare bus stop (**34km**). On your left is a 180-degree turning (SP: M2565/Colmiane/Valdeblore). Proceeding with extreme caution at what can be a dangerous turning, dismounting and crossing on foot if assessed safer, turn left to take the M2565 and start the climb to the Col Saint Martin. ◀

The Col Saint Martin is 16.2km at an average of 6.4%.

The road now climbs steeply via hairpins and tunnels, heading to the attractive communities of Valdeblore. Enter **Valdeblore-La Bolline** (**42.1km**) and cross straight over the mini-roundabout (SP: M2565/Saint-Martin-Vésubie), continuing on the M2565 and passing through the other villages of Valdeblore. Enter the Valdeblore-La Colmiane ski station and crest the **Col Saint Martin** (**50.4km**).

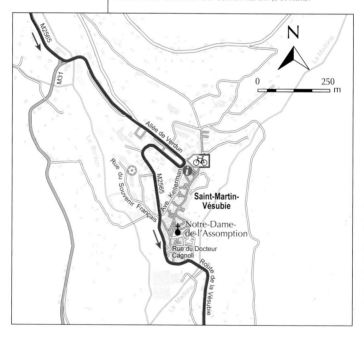

Situated between the Tinée and Vésubie valleys, **Valdeblore** is a collection of three villages, one isolated hamlet and the purpose-built La Colmiane ski resort. While La Colmiane can be a little dispiriting, particularly in early summer when it can be all but deserted, the narrow and cobblestoned streets of the three villages – La Bolline, La Roche and Saint-Dalmas, which united in 1669 to form a single municipality – are attractive and worth exploring should time allow. The Musée du Terroir in Saint-Dalmas tells the history of agricultural life in the area.

Proceed through Valdeblore-La Colmiane, remaining on the M2565. At the roundabout after the small strip of cafés and bars (many, if not all, of which are likely to be closed) go straight on (SP: M2565/Saint-Martin-Vésubie). The road now descends, the high peaks of the Mercantour coming in and out of view as the road twists

Culinary delights await in the backstreets of Saint-Martin-Vésubie

and turns, with Saint-Martin-Vésubie visible below. Enter **Saint-Martin-Vésubie** (**57.6km**). Cross the bridge over the Boréon river and follow signs for Centre Ville. The stage finish is Place du Général de Gaulle, by the town's distinctive terracotta-painted and green-shuttered Hôtel de Ville (**58.7km**).

SAINT-MARTIN-VÉSUBIE

Located at the confluence of the Boréon and Madone de Fenestre mountain streams, which combine to form the Vésubie river, the once-fortified Saint-Martin-Vésubie is an attractive town with a resplendent Hôtel de Ville dominating its central plane-tree-shaded square – the Place du Général de Gaulle.

The locals dub this area 'the Switzerland of Nice' because of the surrounding high peaks. As such, modern-day Saint-Martin-Vésubie markets itself as a hub for outdoor pursuits. As well as being on the RdGA, the town has a number of easily accessible hiking trails that lead into the mountains. Other summer activities available here include canyoning, fishing and horse riding. Some 9km north of the town, on the Lac du Boréon, is Le Parc Alpha, a sanctuary and education centre dedicated to the Mercantour wolf population. There is also a Nordic Centre, where there are climbing walls as well as ski trails for winter exploration.

Saint-Martin-Vésubie's charm lies in the many narrow and steep streets that are begging to be explored and hours can be happily spent here just meandering. Places of interest include the Maison du Coiffeur – a typical Alpine medieval house – and the Notre-Dame-de-l'Assomption church. From autumn to early summer the church shelters the 12th-century statue of Notre-Dame de Fenestre. Made of Lebanese cedar, the statue depicting the Madonna and child is carried in procession to its summer sanctuary at the foot of the Gélas peak.

Be sure to keep looking down as you wander the town's streets: mountain water tumbles down a central gutter, or *gargouille*, on the Rue du Docteur Cagnoli, the town's skinny main thoroughfare, where old balconied buildings now host pleasing shops and restaurants.

STAGE 13

Saint-Martin-Vésubie to Sospel

Start	Place du Général de Gaulle, Saint-Martin-Vésubie (970m)
Finish	Place de la Cabraïa, Sospel (353m)
Distance	52km (32¼ miles)
Total ascent	1570m
Total descent	2187m
Maximum elevation	1616m
Major passes	Col de Turini (1604m)
Refreshments	Roquebillière (8km), La Bollène-Vésubie (15.2km), Col de Turini (27.4km), Moulinet (38.5km)

After descending through the Vésubie valley, Stage 13 kicks up through La Bollène-Vésubie, heading for the Col de Turini, a quite spectacular balcony road made famous by its use in the Monte Carlo Rally. The Turini is a difficult and technical test and represents the final major climb of the route. From its summit it is a 25km descent to the picturesque riverside town of Sospel. The end of the route is now near and a sense of the Mediterranean is palpable, with olive trees appearing and the smell of pine pervading the air.

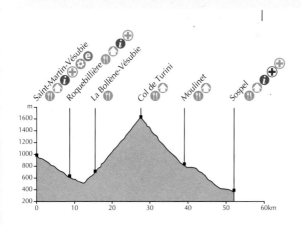

Rated highly for white-water rafting, the 46km Vésubie river rises in the Mercantour, near the Italian border, and flows into the Var some 5km north of La Roquette-sur-Var.

From Saint-Martin-Vésubie's Place du Général de Gaulle, with the main façade of the Hôtel de Ville on your right and the Hotel des Alpes and the small tourist office behind you, proceed along Route de la Vésubie, immediately passing the small post office on your left. Exit Saint-Martin-Vésubie (**1.3km**) and follow the M2565 as it descends through the Vésubie valley. ◄

Enter **Roquebillière** (**8km**). At the mini-roundabout take the third exit (SP: M2565/Belvédère/Nice). Note:

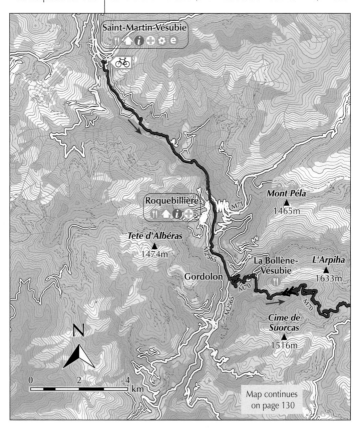

Map continues
on page 130

do not cross the bridge onto the M69 which is also sign-posted 'Nice'. Shortly after passing through Gordolon the road splits. With caution pick up the left-hand feeder lane to take the left-hand turning (SP: M70/La Bollène-Vésubie/Turini), taking additional care when crossing the oncoming traffic (**12.4km**).

The M70 climbs to the top of the Col de Turini, passing through the attractive town of **La Bollène-Vésubie** (**15.2km**) en route to the Turini forest. ▶

La Bollène-Vésubie, La Boulèna in the Niçois dialect, used to be attached to the Earldom of Nice. Its residents are known as the Boulenasc.

Measuring 15.2km at an average of 7.2% from the turn onto the M70, the **Col de Turini** is one of the highlights of the RdGA. While far from being the highest pass in the southern Alps, this spectacular climb has been made famous by its inclusion in the Monte Carlo Rally. First organised in 1911, the event

The famous hairpins of the Col de Turini make for fantastic cycling

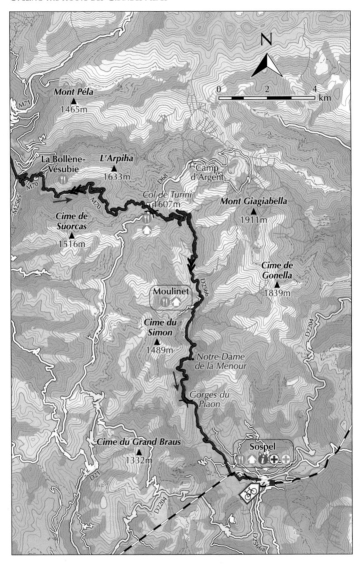

is the oldest on the World Rally Championship calendar and was first used to promote Monte Carlo as a tourist destination, with competitors starting out from numerous European cities and gathering in Monaco. The Turini was first included in the rally in 1961, with former driver John Davenport calling it 'possibly the most famous 23km of road in rally history'. The stage used to be run at night, the beams of powerful headlights piercing the darkness, leading to the nickname 'the night of the long knives'.

From La Bollène-Vésubie the Turini twists and turns upwards for another 12km, climbing steeply through the hairpins that punctuate the Turini forest, making for an enjoyable if unrelenting ascent. There is a real sense of the approaching Mediterranean now, with spruce and larch trees on the ascent soon to be replaced with olive trees and maritime pines on the descent. ▶

At the top of the Turini there are bars and restaurants popular with car enthusiasts who come to drive the pass.

Traverse the top of the **Col de Turini** (**27.4km**) by passing to the right and taking the road to the left of the stone fountain (SP: M2566/Moulinet/Sospel).

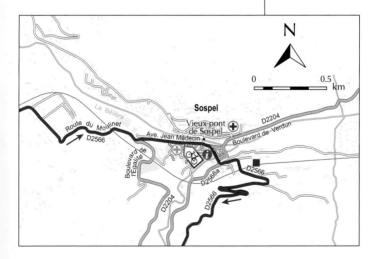

The Notre-Dame de la Ménour is situated on the descent of the Turini

The following descent is steep and technical, the narrow ribbon of road switchbacking down the mountain. Proceed through the colourful community of **Moulinet** (**38.5km**), an attractive collection of buildings, their paint now faded, later passing under the stone viaduct that leads to the Notre-Dame de la Ménour (**42km**).

Situated just south of Moulinet, the **Notre-Dame de la Ménour** is strikingly positioned above the Bévéra valley. The small baroque chapel dates from the 12th century and has been designated a protected site since 1937. The chapel is reached via a 17th-century three-span viaduct, which bridges the road, and a long stone staircase.

The long and twisting balcony road descent continues through the dramatic Gorges du Piaon and beyond. At length enter **Sospel** (**51.3km**) and pass under a railway bridge. At a stop sign turn left (SP: D2204/Centre Ville/Menton) and proceed along the tree-lined Avenue Jean Médecin. The Place de la Cabraïa, the stage finish, is on your right, immediately after passing a pharmacy (**51.9km**).

SOSPEL

Just 20km or so from the Mediterranean, the vibrant town of Sospel lies in the heart of the Bévéra valley within easy reach of both sea and mountain. It is an enjoyable place to spend time soaking up the relaxed atmosphere and refuelling in agreeable restaurants and bars.

Medieval Sospel prospered thanks to its positioning on the salt route between Nice and Turin. Traders paid a toll to use the bridge to cross the Bévéra river, which runs through the town, lining the municipality's pockets.

First references to a bridge in the town have been traced to 1217, although the presence of a nearby chapel – thought to date from the 11th century and which was later dedicated to Saint-Nicolas, patron saint of travellers, merchants and bridges in the Middle Ages – leaves some to speculate that there was a bridge here before the 13th century. The bridge was rebuilt in stone in 1522, although much of it was destroyed during the German retreat of 1944 and later reconstructed to its original design. Over the years the bridge's central tower has been used variously for collecting tolls, as a residence and as a place of business.

The old town, which spans both sides of the river, is delightful to walk around, even if the colourful houses lining the river are perhaps not all they appear to be. Some are painted using the *trompe-l'œil* technique, creating the illusion of doors, windows and balconies where none actually exist.

The colourful houses of Sospel bring an air of Mediterranean life to the RdGA

STAGE 14
Sospel to Nice

Start	Place de la Cabraïa, Sospel (353m)
Finish	Promenade des Anglais, Nice (8m)
Distance	56km (34¾ miles)
Total ascent	1000m
Total descent	1345m
Maximum elevation	719m
Major passes	Col de Castillon (706m); Col d'Èze (507m)
Refreshments	Menton (18.5km), La Turbie (33.2km), Col de Villefranche (48.3km)

From Sospel, the final stage of the RdGA heads to the coast via the Col de Castillon. After visiting the colourful coastal town of Menton, the route swings west, heading for the Cote d'Azur's popular Grande Corniche and the Col d'Èze, the final climb of the route. Views over Monaco, Beaulieu-sur-Mer and Cap Ferrat can be enjoyed from upon high before the road finally reaches Nice for a blast along the Promenade des Anglais and a well-deserved celebratory dip in the Med.

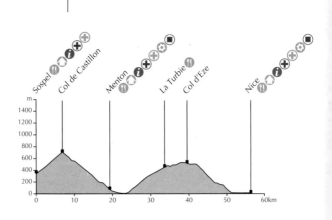

From Sospel's Place de la Cabraïa proceed along Avenue Jean Médecin with the Bévéra river on your left. Pass the old bridge and then take the turning signposted 'D2566/ Menton/Castillon'. At the roundabout take the exit signposted 'D2566/Col de Castillon/RdGA'. Follow the road around to the right and go over the level crossing to climb the Col de Castillon. ▶

Climbing through olive groves as it gains height, the Col de Castillon is 7km at an average of 5.1%.

At the summit of the **Col de Castillon (7km)** follow the road around to the left and pass through a short tunnel (SP:Castillon/Menton). Descend through hairpins to a junction and turn left (SP: Castillon/Menton).

The old village of **Castillon**, originally situated near the pass, was destroyed by an earthquake in 1887. Rebuilt lower down the hillside, the new village was then destroyed in World War 2. Again rebuilt, the village won the prize for France's most beautiful village in 1952. Today it has a reputation for arts and crafts, with creatives joining together in the 'Arcades du Serre' syndicate.

The hillsides of the Col de Castillon

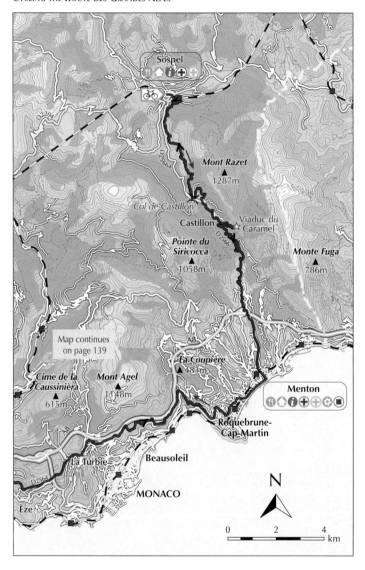

Map continues on page 139

136

The rooftops of Menton with the Mediterranean beyond

From here the traffic is likely to get busier, the D2566 being the main route from the north into Menton. The road dives down towards the coast, traversing the Carei valley and passing the 13-arch Caramel viaduct. ▶

At the roundabout on the outskirts of Menton go straight on (second exit) to remain on the D2566 and at length enter **Menton** (**18.5km**). Pass under the A8 Autoroute and at the next roundabout take the first exit (SP: D2566/Centre Ville). Shortly after, pick up the quieter Route de Sospel, just to the right of the D2566, and follow, occasionally rejoining the main road, until you reach a stop sign where it permanently rejoins the main road (**20.4km**). Proceed on the D2566, passing straight over two roundabouts, to reach the Casino Barrière.

Just 3km or so from the Italian border, **Menton** is dubbed the pearl of France. It is busy and lively with an old town that is a delight, large ochre-coloured, shuttered houses crowding the streets. The town is linked with Jean Cocteau, the author, filmmaker, artist and poet whose most famous work is *Les Enfants Terribles*. Cocteau decorated buildings in Menton, including the town's *Salle des Mariages*. The town celebrates his work in two museums – the

Built for the Menton–Sospel tramway in 1912, the Caramel viaduct was deliberately detached from the mountainside, making it easy to destroy in times of war, to hamper the progress of enemy forces.

Menton's Musée du Bastion which houses works by Jean Cocteau

Musée Jean Cocteau and the Musée du Bastion – although at the time of writing the former had been closed for a number of years due to storm damage suffered in 2018.

At the roundabout in front of the casino take the first exit (SP: D6007/Nice/Monaco). Proceed along the busy D6007 until you reach a palm-tree-planted roundabout. Take the second exit (SP: Monaco/Nice/Centre Ville) to enter **Roquebrune-Cap-Martin (23km)**. Proceed along Avenue Jean Monnet. Pass under a railway line and at the next roundabout take the third exit (SP: D123/Monaco). This road soon rejoins the D6007. Pass the Saint-Joseph church on the left and at the next roundabout take the second exit (SP: D6007/Monaco/Vieux Village). The road now climbs more steeply and at the next roundabout (**25.4km**) take the first exit (SP: D2564/La Turbie). The distinctive form of Monaco will soon come into sight as you gain height. Follow the ever-climbing D2564 Grande Corniche through **La Turbie** all the way to the **Col d'Èze** (**39.5km**): the final climb of the route but one that passes with little fanfare. ◀

Three corniche roads traverse this remarkable coastline – the Grande, Moyenne and Inférieure. This route uses the Grande Corniche, the highest. If misty, consider using one of the lower roads.

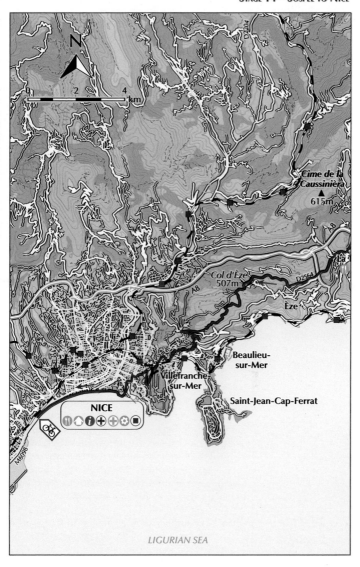

Remaining on the same road, descend towards the Col des Quatre Chemins and at the restaurant La Chaumière (**44.1km**) take the 180-degree left turn (SP: M33/Villefranche/Beaulieu) to immediately enter **Villefranche-sur-Mer**.

From Roquebrune the **Col d'Èze** is 15km at an average of 3%. It is famous for its inclusion in the Paris–Nice cycling race. Dubbed the Race to the Sun, and held every February, for more than 20 years it climaxed with an individual time trial from Nice to the Col d'Èze. During the 1980s it was a popular stage with Irish riders: Sean Kelly is a five-time winner of the stage while Stephen Roche won it four times.

Descend to a junction and turn right (SP: M6007/Beaulieu/RdGA). Follow the road through Villefranche and Carne d'Or to enter **Nice** (**48.3km**). Continue descending on the M6007, passing Parc Municipal Castel des Deux Rois on your left, to reach Place Max Barel. Take the third exit (SP: Nice-Centre) onto Rue Barla and then, almost immediately, take the first left onto Rue Arson (SP: Port). Follow Rue Arson until it meets Place Île-de-Beauté (**51km**). Turn right, passing in front of the Notre-Dame du Port church before following the road to the left. ◄

The Notre-Dame du Port was declared a historical monument in 1991. Neoclassical in style, it was built between 1840 and 1853. Its 4 large columns were added 40 years later.

Pick up the cycle path to the left that runs along the seafront, riding alongside Quai Rauba Capeu and Quai Etats-Unis (**52km**) before arriving alongside the Promenade des Anglais, which extends for some 7km around Nice's seafront. All that remains is a final easy cruise beside the sea to complete your epic journey. How far you go is your choice, although the stage distance is based on continuing to the promenade's halfway point before dismounting for the final time (**56km**).

Locals enjoying a ride along the Promenade des Anglais

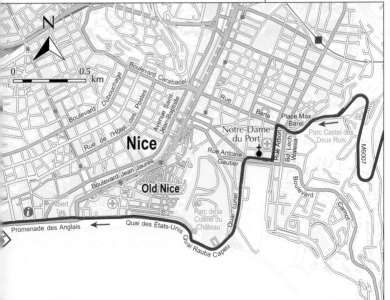

VARIANT 1
Saint-Jean-de-Sixt to Villard-sur-Doron

Start	Tourist office, Saint-Jean-de-Sixt (963m)
Finish	Hôtel La Cascade, Villard-sur-Doron (712m)
Distance	127km (79 miles)
Total ascent	1535m
Total descent	1786m
Maximum elevation	963m
Major passes	Col de Bluffy (630m); Col de Leschaux (897m); Col du Frêne (950m)
Refreshments	Thônes (8.5km), Annecy (28km), Lescheraines (59km), La Motte-en-Bauges (61.5km), Saint-Pierre-d'Albigny (85km)), Albertville (107km)

Variant 1 avoids the Col d'Aravis and Col des Saisies, heading instead to the spectacular lakeside town of Annecy. From there a climb through the Bauges national park via the Col de Leschaux and Col du Frêne is followed by a sharp and technical descent to Saint-Pierre-d'Albigny. A ride through vineyards and sleepy villages to Albertville follows before the road rises for the final 15km to Villard-sur-Doron, where it rejoins the main route. Due to its length, it is recommended you undertake this variant in two stages, with options for an overnight stay in and around La Motte-en-Bauges and Saint-Pierre-d'Albigny.

From the roundabout by the tourist office in Saint-Jean-de-Sixt take the exit signposted 'D909/Thônes'.

Follow the D909. Note: do not take the D16 exit at the large roundabout (**14.8km**) which is signposted Annecy. Instead, take the second exit (SP: D909/Alex/Lac d'Annecy). At the junction at the bottom of the descent from the **Col de Bluffy** (**22.8km**) turn right (SP: Annecy).

At Veyrier-du-Lac pick up the cycle path bordering the lake (**23.9km**). Follow it through and out of Annecy until you reach the church in **Sévrier** (**33.8km**).

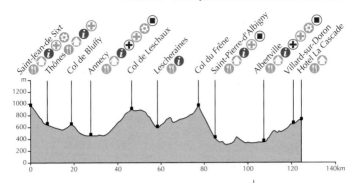

Turn right off the cycle path. Proceed to the junction with the road. Turn left onto the D1508. At next roundabout take first exit (SP: Leschaux). Follow the D912. ▸

At the **Col de Leschaux** (**46.5km**) turn left then turn right onto the D10 (SP: Bellecombe-en-Bauges). Note: this road later becomes the D61.

The Col de Leschaux from Sévrier measures 11.9km at an average of 3.7%.

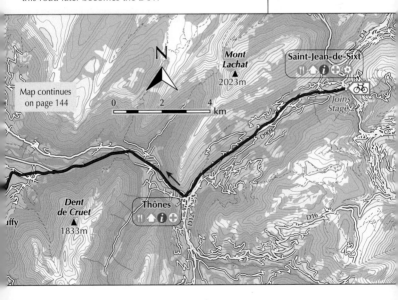

Annecy

Mont Veyrier
1291m

D16

Veyrier-
du-Lac

Col de Bluffy
639m

Bluffy

Den
de Cr

1833

Sévrier

Menthon-
Saint-Bernard

D909

Lac d'Annecy

Saint-Jorioz

Talloires

D1508

D909

D912

Crêt de Châtillon
1699m

Leschaux

Col de Leschaux
897m

Roc des
Boeufs
1774m

D5

Bellecombe-
en-Bauges

D1508

N

D912

Arith

Lescheraines

La Motte-
en-Bauges

Mont Julioz
▲1680m

Map continues
on page 146

0   2   4
                     km

Le Trélod
▲2181m

Le

Giant, multicoloured, inflatable balls afloat on Lake Annecy

Shortly after **Bellecombe-en-Bauges (53km)** pick up the D61A by continuing straight on (SP: Lescheraines) and continue to the junction. Turn left to rejoin the D912 (**56km**).

Proceed to the junction with the D911 (**57.5km**) and turn left (SP: Lescheraines). Follow the D911 to the Col du Frêne (**77.4km**) and **Saint-Pierre-d'Albigny** beyond (**85km**). ▸

At the junction with the D201 (**85km**) turn left. Pass vineyards and continue through numerous villages until you reach the junction with the D990 (**102km**). Turn left.

Enter **Albertville**. Follow signs for Centre Ville, passing Parc Aubry onto Rue de la République. Just after the pharmacy at No 42, turn right onto Rue Gambetta. Note: ignore No Entry sign; cyclists are permitted – but take care with oncoming traffic.

Emerge opposite the bridge (**108km**). Cross over the bridge. At the mini-roundabout take the third exit (SP: D925/Venthon/Beaufort).

Proceed on the D925 for 21km until you reach the Hotel Restaurant La Cascade (1km beyond Villard-sur-Doron), where you will join Stage 3 of the main route (**127km**).

From the village of École, the Col du Frêne is 8km. While much of the climb is gentle the last 2km averages 6%.

145

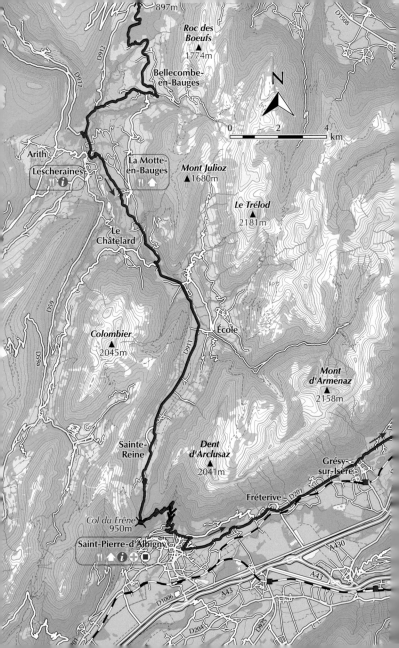

897m

Roc des Boeufs
▲ 1774m

Bellecombe-
en-Bauges

N

0   2   4
km

Arith

Lescheraines

La Motte-
en-Bauges

Mont Julioz
▲ 1680m

Le Trélod
▲ 2181m

Le
Châtelard

Colombier
▲ 2045m

École

*Mont
d'Armenaz*
▲ 2158m

Sainte-
Reine

*Dent
d'Arclusaz*
▲ 2041m

Grésy-
sur-Isère

Fréterive

Col du Frêne
950m

Saint-Pierre-d'Albigny

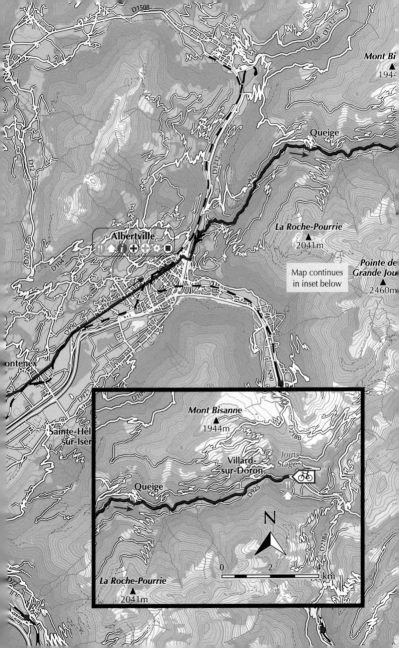

VARIANT 2
Bourg-Saint-Maurice to Saint-Michel-de-Maurienne

Start	Rond-Point des Grands Cols, Bourg-Saint-Maurice (815m)
Finish	Rue du Galibier, Saint-Michel-de-Maurienne (717m)
Distance	105.25km (65½ miles)
Total ascent	2330m
Total descent	2428m
Maximum elevation	1995m
Major passes	Col de la Madeleine (1993m)
Refreshments	Landry (6.9km), Aime-la-Plagne (14km), Moûtiers (28.1km), Petit-Coeur La Léchère (34.6km), Col de la Madeleine (62.7km), Saint-François-Longchamp (70.5km), La Chambre (81.5km), Saint-Jean-de-Maurienne (93km)

Avoiding the Col de l'Iseran, Variant 2 departs Bourg-Saint-Maurice via an attractive cycle path alongside the Isère river, joining the road at Aime-la-Plagne. After an unpleasant stretch along the busy and fast N90, where extra care is needed, the route traverses bustling Moûtiers before heading away from the main road to scale the long and difficult Col de la Madeleine. A descent through the ski stations that dot the mountain's southern flank follows, before a ride through the busy Maurienne valley to the finish town of Saint-Michel-de-Maurienne. Due to its length, it is recommended you undertake this variant in two stages, with options for an overnight stay in Saint-François-Longchamp or La Chambre.

From the Rond-Point des Grands Cols in Bourg-Saint-Maurice take the exit behind the railway station, towards the funicular, onto the Avenue de l'Arc-en-Ciel.

Pass the funicular. At the end of the avenue turn left onto the D84C (SP: Les Arcs). Almost immediately, shortly before a bridge, turn right off the D84C. The Isère river is to the left and the main railway line to the right.

VARIANT 2 – BOURG-SAINT-MAURICE TO SAINT-MICHEL-DE-MAURIENNE

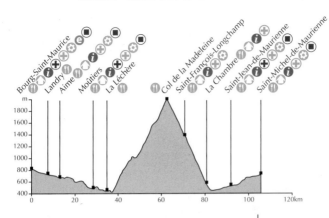

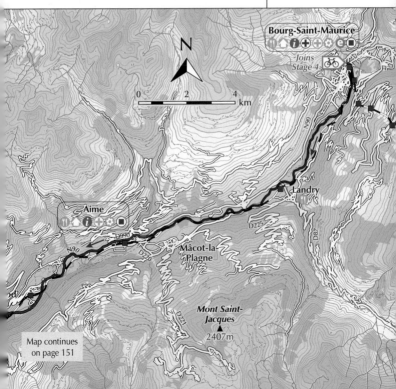

Map continues
on page 151

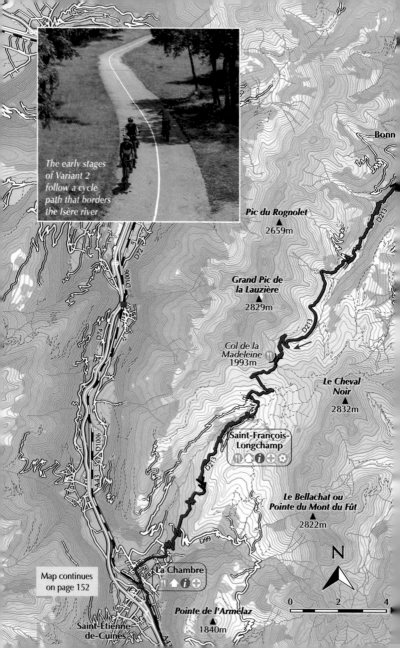

The early stages of Variant 2 follow a cycle path that borders the Isère river

Bonn

Pic du Rognolet
▲
2659m

Grand Pic de la Lauzière
▲
2829m

Col de la Madeleine
1993m

Le Cheval Noir
▲
2832m

Saint-François-Longchamp

Le Bellachat ou Pointe du Mont du Fût
▲
2822m

Map continues on page 152

La Chambre

Pointe de l'Armélaz
▲
1840m

Saint-Étienne-de-Cuines

N

0   2   4

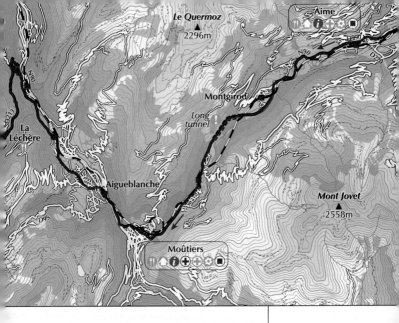

At the junction with the D220 turn left. Take the cycle path over the river, immediately following the cycle path down and to the left before turning sharply right to pass back under the bridge (**2.4km**). With the river now on your right, follow the cycle path for 11km.

At the Rive Gauche restaurant (**13.4km**) turn right over the wooden bridge then quickly turn left to the D220. Turn right and follow the cycle path alongside the D220 into **Aime**. (Note: the D220 becomes the D990 as you traverse the town.)

Pass through Aime, following signs for Moûtiers. As you exit Aime (**15.6km**), take the slip road for the N90. Follow the N90 for some 12km towards Moûtiers. ▶

At length turn right off the N90 onto the D990 (SP: D990/ Moûtiers-Centre) and enter **Moûtiers** (**28.2km**). Follow the D990 signposts for Gare Routière. Pass the bus station and continue to a small roundabout. Take the first exit (SP: Albertville). At the next roundabout take the second exit, following a signpost for Aigueblanche with a small moped symbol next to it.

The N90 is a fast and busy road that includes the unpleasant 1.6km Tunnel du Siaix (21.4km). Extreme caution and good lighting are required.

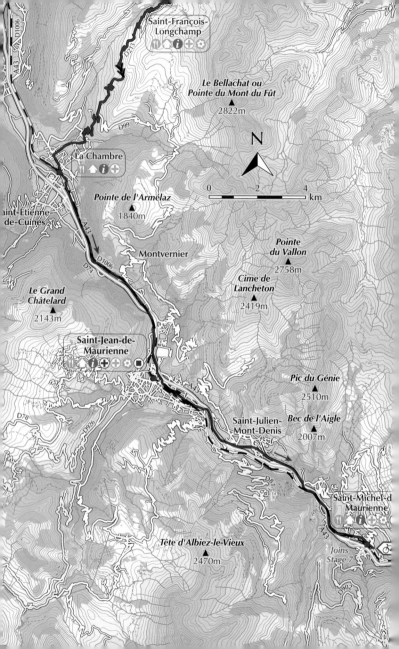

Saint-François-Longchamp

Le Bellachat ou
Pointe du Mont du Fût
2822m

N

0   2   4
km

La Chambre

Saint-Étienne-de-Cuines

Pointe de l'Armélaz
1840m

Montvernier

Pointe
du Vallon
2758m

Cime de
Lancheton
2419m

Le Grand
Châtelard
2143m

Saint-Jean-de-Maurienne

Pic du Génie
2510m

Bec de l'Aigle
2007m

Saint-Julien-Mont-Denis

Saint-Michel-de-Maurienne

Tête d'Albiez-le-Vieux
2470m

Joins
Stage 7

Pass under the motorway and enter **Aigueblanche** (**31km**). At the pharmacy turn left (SP: D94/Valmorel). Cross the bridge and exit the town via three roundabouts, always following the D97A/Albertville. Exit Aigueblanche and remain on the D97A, which soon merges with the D97.

Enter **La Léchère**/Petit-Coeur (**34.6km**). At the roundabout take the second exit (SP: D97/Notre-Dame-de-Briançon). Note: do not take the first exit despite it being signposted 'Col de la Madeleine'.

At the junction with the D213 (**37.5km**) turn left. Follow the D213 to the Col de la Madeleine (**62.7km**). ▶

From the **Col de la Madeleine** continue on the D213 for the long and steep descent into **La Chambre** (**81.5km**). ▶

At the T-junction opposite the Hotel L'Eterlou turn left (SP: D213/Toutes Directions). At the roundabout after Saint-Arve's small railway station take the first exit (SP: D213/Saint-Jean-de-Maurienne). Pass over the railway. At the next roundabout take the third exit (SP: D1006/Saint-Jean-de-Maurienne) (**83.5km**).

The Col de la Madeleine is listed as 25.3km at an average of 6.2%, but the road actually rises all the way from Aigueblanche, adding 3km more of (gentle) climbing.

La Chambre is named after a family of nobility who owned land in the area during the Middle Ages and were rivals of the House of Savoy.

Road graffiti from past Tour de France remains a common sight

Remain on the D1006, following the Arc river and ignoring a turning to Saint-Jean-de-Maurienne (**90.6km**) unless taking the Croix de Fer option noted below. At length continue through the industrial outskirts of **Saint-Jean-de-Maurienne** (**93km**), remaining, at all times, on the D1006 towards Saint-Michel-de-Maurienne.

At length pass Hotel du Galibier (**104km**). At the roundabout take the first exit (SP: D1006/Turin) to enter **Saint-Michel-de-Maurienne**. At the next roundabout take the second exit, remaining on the D1006 (SP: Modane/ Centre Ville).

Proceed to traffic lights at the junction with the D902. Turn right to join Stage 7 of the main route for the climb of the Col du Télégraphe (**105.3km**).

Two alternative routes to the above can be taken to meet Variant 4. These should be considered if it is known the Col du Galibier is closed.

- Col du Glandon: From the roundabout at the 83.5km point take the second exit (SP: D927 Albertville/Turin). Follow the D927 to the Col du Glandon (21.3km at 6.9%). Then descend briefly to the junction with the D926. Turn right to join Variant 4 for the descent to Allemont.

- Col de la Croix de Fer: At the 90.6km point take the exit to Saint-Jean-de-Maurienne (SP: D906/Col de la Croix de Fer). Follow signs for Gare SNCF and then Vallée de l'Arvan. At the Rond-Point des Arves take the D926 to join Variant 4 and climb the Col de la Croix de Fer.

VARIANT 3

Val Cenis Lanslevillard to Briançon

Start	Hotel L'Etoile des Neiges, Val Cenis Lanslevillard (1464m)
Finish	Rond-Point des Alpes, Briançon (1259m)
Distance	95.5km (59½ miles)
Total ascent	2355m
Total descent	2560m
Maximum elevation	2098m
Major passes	Col du Mont-Cenis (2081m); Col de Montgenevre (1850m)
Refreshments	Col du Mont Cenis (9.4km), Bar Cenisio (25.6km), Susa (38.9km), Exilles (51.5km), Oulx (63.2km), Montgenèvre (82km)

Variant 3 avoids the Col du Galibier, instead heading to Briançon from Val Cenis Lanslevillard via the Col du Mont Cenis and Montgenèvre. While there is much to enjoy on the climb of Mont Cenis and the subsequent descent into Italy, this variant includes a long stretch of the SS24, a major and busy road with long tunnels. Accordingly, it is recommended that this variant should be avoided if possible and only considered if the Col du Galibier is known to be closed. Even then, Variant 4 should be considered instead: a longer but preferable option provided the Col de la Croix de Fer and the Col du Glandon are open. Due to its length, it is recommended you undertake this variant in two stages, with options for an overnight stay in Exilles or Oulx.

From the Hotel L'Etoile des Neiges in Val Cenis Lanslevillard cross the small bridge over the Arc river (SP: D115/Col du Mont Cenis).

At the junction with the D1006 (**1.5km**) turn left and follow road to the **Col du Mont Cenis**. ▶

Continue on the D1006 to the Lac du Mont Cenis and beyond. Cross the border into Italy (**22.5km**), where the road becomes the SS25.

The Col du Mont Cenis (9.8km/6.9%) is a pleasing climb on a pine-shaded road that doubles up as a ski run in winter. At the top, the Relais du Col offers refreshments.

Map continues
on page 159

Descend on the SS25, traversing **Bar Cenisio** (**25.6km**), Moloretto (**29.6km**), **San Martino** (**30.9km**) and Giaglione (**35.1km**) to enter the town of **Susa** (**38.9km**).

Just 1km to go of this wonderful climb

At the first set of main traffic lights turn right onto the Via Mazzini (SP: Centro). Pass the Museo Diocesano and cross a bridge. Continue through Piazza IV Novembre and beyond, navigating narrow streets, always continuing

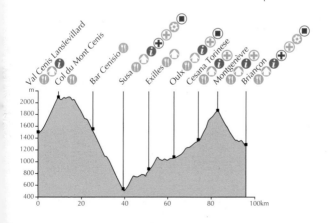

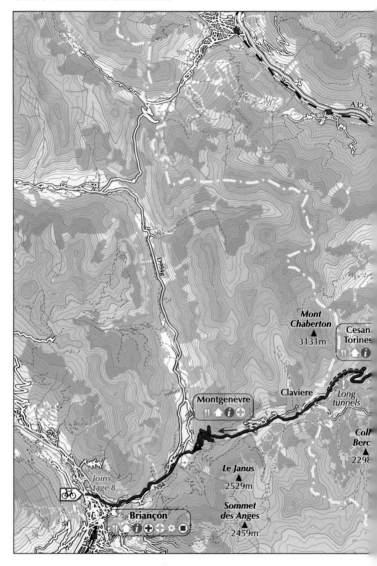

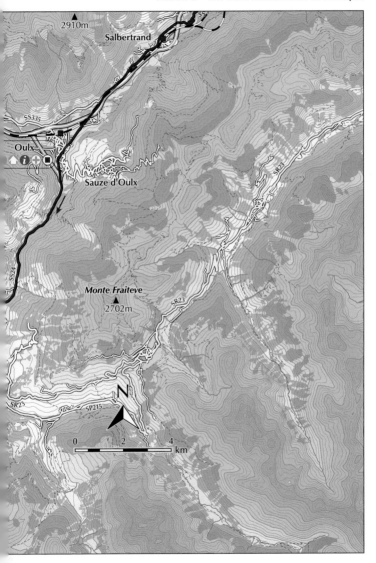

The SS24 is a wide and heavily trafficked road punctuated by tunnels where lights are compulsory. Extreme caution is demanded; it rises, sharply in places, for much of the 40km to Montgenèvre.

The descent from Montgenèvre proceeds sharply through a series of tight bends affording wonderful views over the Briançonnais. There is a short uphill section as the road approaches Briançon.

straight on until you reach the junction with the SS24. Turn right (SP: Francia/Monginevro). ◀

Shortly after the SS24 76km road marking look for a junction before a short tunnel. Take the turning to the left of the tunnel (SP: Gad/Oulx Centro). Traverse **Oulx** (**63.5km**) and remain on the SS24.

Enter **Cesana Torinese** (**73.2km**). At the first roundabout take the exit (SP: SS24/Claviere/Francia/Cesana Centro). Traverse and exit Cesana Torinese, remaining on the SS24, following signposts for Claviere/Francia.

At the roundabout on entering **Claviere** (**79.6km**), take the second exit (SP: Claviere Centro). Note: ignore the first exit signed 'Monginevro'. Continue through the town to emerge at a junction. Turn left (SP: Francia/Monginevro) to rejoin the SS24.

Pass back into France, where the road becomes the N94.

Remain on the N94 to **Montgenèvre** (**81.7km**). At the roundabout by the Napoleon obelisk take the second exit onto the Route d'Italie (SP: Montgenèvre/Office de Tourisme). Note: do not take the third exit signposted to Briançon, which heads through a tunnel forbidden to cyclists.

Proceed along Route d'Italie. Emerge onto a roundabout and take the first exit (SP: Briançon). Exit Montgenèvre (**84.1km**). ◀

Descend to **Briançon** (**93.7km**). At the first roundabout take the exit onto Avenue Baldenberger (SP: Toutes Directions). Continue onto Avenue Professor Forgues (SP: Grenoble/Serre Chevalier) to emerge onto the roundabout Rond-Point des Alpes, where you will join the main route at the Stage 8 finish point (**95.6km**).

VARIANT 4

Saint-Michel-de-Maurienne to Col du Lautaret

Start	Rue du Général Ferrié, Saint-Michel-de-Maurienne (717m)
Finish	Col du Lautaret (2058m)
Distance	119km (74 miles)
Total ascent	3700m
Total descent	2359m
Maximum elevation	2064m
Major passes	Col de la Croix de Fer (2064m)/Col du Glandon (1924m); Col du Lautaret (2058m)
Refreshments	Saint-Jean-de-Maurienne (11km), Saint-Jean-d'Arves (32km), Col de la Croix de Fer (42km), Allemont (70km), Le Bourg-d'Oisans (80km), Le Freney-d'Oisans (92km), La Grave (108km), Villar-d'Arène (112km), Col du Lautaret (119km).

Variant 4 offers another option for avoiding the Col du Galibier, instead proceeding along the Maurienne valley before tackling another giant of the Tour de France: the Col de la Croix de Fer. The road then descends, passing the Col du Glandon and the Grand Maison and Verney lakes, before entering Allemont (sometimes spelled Allemond). A blast along the valley road follows to Le Bourg-d'Oisans, where you can make a diversion from the route to take in the famous 21-hairpin climb to Alpe d'Huez. From Le Bourg-d'Oisans there is a long drag up through the Romanche Valley to the top of the Col du Lautaret. Due to its length, it is recommended you undertake this variant in two stages, with options for an overnight stay in Allemont or Le Bourg-d'Oisans.

At the traffic lights on the junction of Rue du Général Ferrié and Rue du Galibier in Saint-Michel-de-Maurienne, proceed along the D1006 in the direction of Saint-Jean-de-Maurienne.

Map continues
on page 164

Col de la
Croix de Fer
2064m

Col du
Glandon
1924m

Fontcouver
la-Toussui

Saint-Sorlin-
d'Arves

Saint-Jean
d'Arves

D91

D926

D526

D926

**Pic
Bunard**
▲
2560m

Lac de Grand'Maison

Les Perrons
▲
2620m

**Le
issiou**
▲
622m

**Côte
Belle**
▲
2395m

*The Grand Maison lake on the
descent towards Allemont*

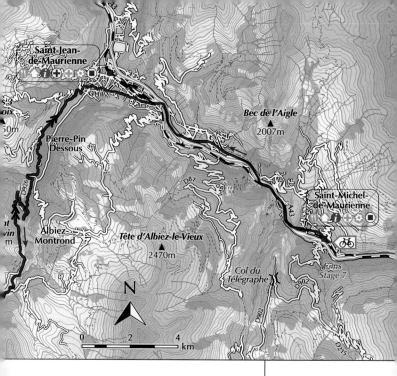

Exit Saint-Michel-de-Maurienne and remain on the D1006. At length cross the bridge over the Arc river (**10.1km**). At the roundabout immediately after, take the second exit (SP: D906/Saint-Jean-de-Maurienne).

Enter **Saint-Jean-de-Maurienne**, remaining on the D906 and navigate two roundabouts, following signs for Vallée de l'Arvan. Note: take care not to take the exit signposted 'Centre Ville' at the second roundabout. After crossing the Arvan river, and immediately after passing Camping des Grands Cols, turn left onto the D110 (SP: Vallée de l'Arvan/Col de la Croix de Fer).

Proceed to the Rond-Point des Clapeys and take the third exit (SP: Vallée de l'Arvan/Col de la Croix de Fer). At the Rond-Point des Arves take the first exit (SP: D926/Vallée de l'Arvan) (**13.5km**) to start the Col de la Croix de Fer. ▶

The 30km Col de la Croix de Fer offers spectacular views over the three peaks of the Aiguilles d'Arves. The climb is as rewarding as it is difficult.

163

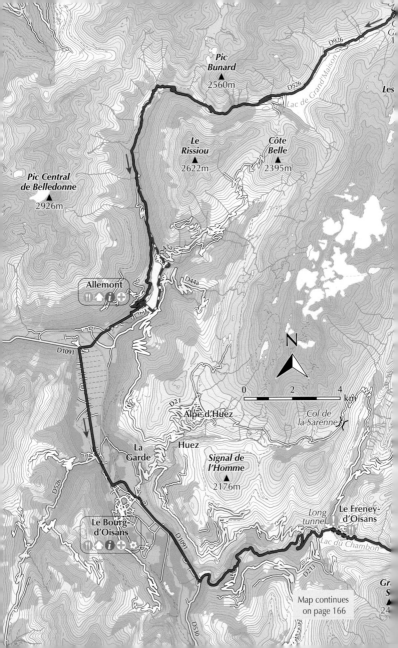

Pic Bunard
2560m

Le Rissiou
2622m

Côte Belle
2395m

Pic Central de Belledonne
2926m

Lac de Grand Maison

D926

D526

Les

D43

D44a

Allemont

D1091

N

0   2   4 km

Alpe d'Huez

Col de la Sarenne

D21

La Garde

Huez

Signal de l'Homme
2176m

D526

Long tunnel

Le Freney-d'Oisans

Le Bourg-d'Oisans

D1091

Lac du Chambon

D213

Gr S 24

D530

Map continues on page 166

Immediately after entering the commune of **Pierre-Pin Dessous** (**16.9km**) turn left to remain on the D926 (SP: D926/Montrond/Col de la Croix de Fer). Note: take care not to inadvertently carry straight on here.

The Col de la Croix de Fer stands under the gaze of the striking Aiguilles d'Arves

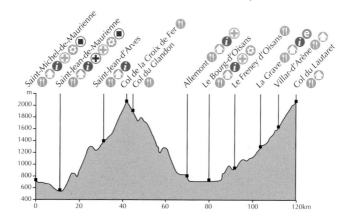

Follow the D926, at length passing through Saint-Sorlin-d'Arves (**35km**), to the top of the **Col de la Croix de Fer**.

From the pass descend sharply towards Allemont, passing a turning on the right that leads to the Col du Glandon and then the Lac de Grand'Maison, where the route crosses into the Isère department and the road becomes the D526. ◀

> The first kilometres of the descent are open with sweeping bends, but the road soon tightens with hairpins that need to be navigated. It also features some long uphill sections.

At length turn right off the D526 (SP: D43/Le Villaret/Allemont Église) (**65.5km**). Note: you can choose to remain on the D526 and enter Allemont via the Barrage du Verney instead.

Enter **Allemont Église** (**68.3km**), remaining on the D43 to the junction with the D526. Turn right and continue to the junction with the D1091 (**73.5km**).

Turn left (SP: D1091/Briançon/Bourg-d'Oisans). Proceed to **Le Bourg-d'Oisans**. At the roundabout at the

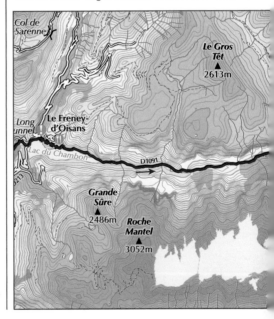

entrance of the town (**79.5km**) take the third exit (SP: D1091/Briançon/L'Alpe d'Huez) to by-pass the main town. Note: a quieter and recommended alternative here is to take the cycle path at the roundabout then at the cycle lane junction soon after, go straight over. At the next junction turn left onto Route du Stade. Follow the road round to the right (SP: Pont de la Romanche). Continue until the road ends. Turn left and cross the bridge. Both options through the town emerge onto the same roundabout.

At the roundabout take the exit towards Briançon (SP: D1091/Briançon/Les Deux Alpes). At Le Clapier d'Auris (**85km**) the road swings round to the left for the start of the Col du Lautaret. ▶

The road to the Lautaret climbs through the villages of **Le Freney-d'Oisans**, Les Freaux, **La Grave** and Villard'Arene. At the top of the **Col du Lautaret**, you will join

From Le Clapier the interminable Col du Lautaret measures 34.2km at 3.8%. The climb is busy and features many dark tunnels. Care and good lights are required.

167

The riders of the Tour de France scale Alpe d'Huez

Stage 8 of the main route (**119km**).

The famous **climb to Alpe d'Huez** is reached from the roundabout at the exit of Le Bourg-d'Oisans. Measuring 13.8km long at an average of 8.1%, l'Alpe d'Huez was first used by the Tour de France in 1952. Then the legendary cyclist Fausto Coppi won the stage on his way to his second overall Tour victory. The Alpe as it is now known in Tour parlance grew to become one of the race's most legendary climbs. Win a Tour stage here and your name is posted on to one of the climb's famous 21 hairpins, with Bernard Hinault and Marco Pantani joining Coppi among those famous names. To ride the 21-hairpins, take the exit signposted 'D211/L'Alpe d'Huez' and follow the D211 to the ski resort. Return to the route by retracing your ride to the roundabout at the exit of Bourg-d'Oisans. Alternatively, if you have a good head for narrow and precipitous roads, traverse the sprawling ski resort, following signs for the Bergers district and the altiport. Pass the altiport and follow the Route du Col de Sarenne, a wild and narrow road, to the Sarenne pass (**9km**). A sharp and technical descent follows to a junction with the D25. Turn right (SP: Mizoen) and follow the D25 to the junction with the D1091. Turn left to pick up the climb to the Col du Lautaret.

VARIANT 5

Guillestre to Barcelonnette

Start	Rond-Point Porte du Queyras, Guillestre (1054m)
Finish	Pont du Plan, Barcelonnette (1140m)
Distance	74.5km (46¼ miles)
Total ascent	860m
Total descent	774m
Maximum elevation	1135m
Major passes	N/A
Refreshments	Embrun (19.5km), Savines-le-Lac (29km), Le Sauze-du-Lac (40.5km), Le Lauzet-Ubaye (54.5km) Les Thuiles (68.5km), Barcelonnette (74.5km)

Avoiding the Col de Vars, Variant 5 heads from Guillestre to Barcelonnette via the busy N94 and the bustling town of Embrun. If the first half of this variant is unpleasant, things improve once you leave the N94 behind at Savines-le-Lac, and the route traverses the resorts that dot the shore of the Serre-Ponçon lake. After passing the remarkable Demoiselles Coiffées de Pontis rock formation, the route descends through a series of hairpins to a bridge over the southern tip of the lake. This is followed by a long drag up through the Ubaye Valley to Barcelonnette.

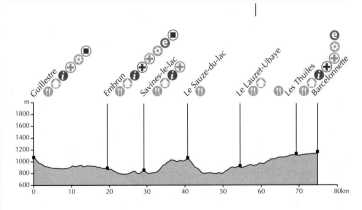

Tête de
l'Hivernet
▲
2823m

Mont Guillaume
▲
2542m

D9

D9

Puy Sanières

D9

Lac de Serre-Ponçon

D3

Savines-le-Lac
🍴 🏠 ℹ️ ➕

N94

D954

Orbanne

Pontis

Pic du
Morgon
▲
2324m

Demoiselles
Coiffées de Pontis

Le Sauze-
du-Lac
🍴

Old/dark
tunnel

D954

Map continues
on page 172

D900B

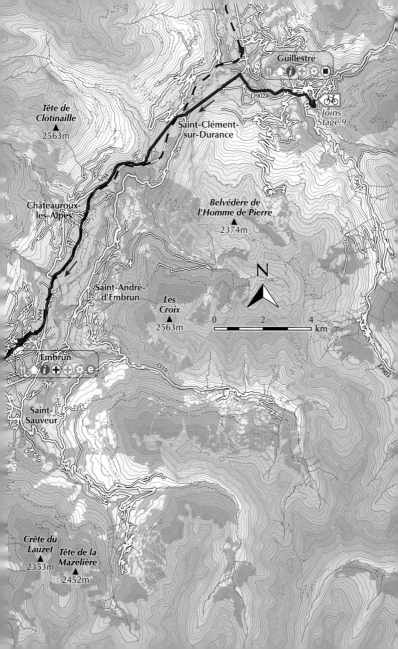

Guillestre

D902a

Joins
Stage 9

Tête de
Clotinaille
2563m

Saint-Clément-
sur-Durance

N94

Châteauroux-
les-Alpes

Belvédère de
l'Homme de Pierre
2374m

N

Saint-André-
d'Embrun

Les
Croix
2563m

0   2   4
km

N94

Embrun

D39

Saint-
Sauveur

D902

Crête du
Lauzet
2353m

Tête de la
Mazelière
2452m

The N94 is the main link between Briançon and Gap. As such it is fast and busy and unpleasant for the cyclist. Extra care is demanded.

At Rond-Point Porte de Queyras take the exit signposted 'D902A/Vars/Risoul/Embrun' to the Rond-Point Le Château (the end point of Stage 9). Take the first exit (SP: D902a/Risoul/Embrun). Proceed out of Guillestre, crossing all roundabouts, always remaining on the D902a, following signs for Embrun until you reach the roundabout with the N94 (**4.4km**). Take the third exit (SP: N94/Gap/Sisteron/Embrun). ◄

Remain on the N94 for some 13km. Shortly after passing a stone viaduct on the left, the road approaches a roundabout (**17.2km**). Take the first exit (SP: D994h/Embrun).

Proceed along the D994h and enter **Embrun** (**19.1km**). Traverse the town, carrying straight on and

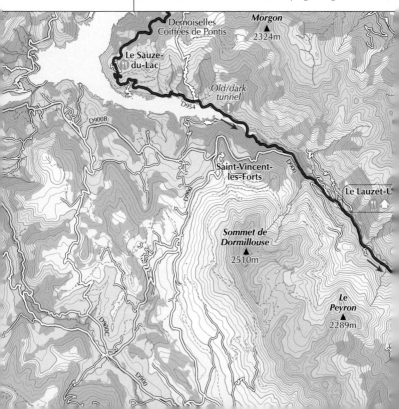

following signs for Gap. Shortly after crossing a stone bridge, the road emerges onto a large roundabout (**22.6km**). Take the second exit (SP: N94/Gap/Lac de Serre-Ponçon) to rejoin the busy N94.

At length enter **Savines-le-Lac** (**29km**). Just before a bridge turn left (SP: D954/Le Sauze-du-Lac/Barcelonnette).

Follow the D954. After you have passed the tiny community of Orbanne (**36.4km**), the striking Demoiselles Coiffées de Pontis will come into view. ▶

The Demoiselles Coiffées de Pontis are a series of tapered columns supporting larger rocks on top, resulting in the 'ladies with hairdos' moniker.

The striking 'ladies with hairdos' (Demoiselles Coiffées de Pontis) tower above the road near Sauze-du-Lac

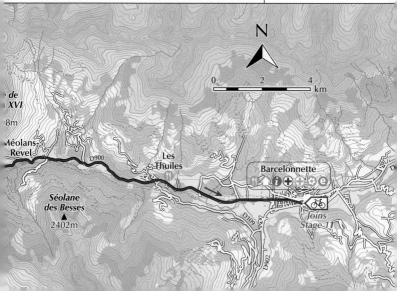

The waters of the Serre-Ponçon lake seem impossibly blue

The Serre-Ponçon lake was constructed between 1955 and 1960 after the flooding of the Durance and Ubaye rivers devastated the area in the mid 1800s.

Pass through the outskirts of **Le Sauze-du-Lac** (**40.6km**) and descend through tight hairpins. The route now passes into the Alpes-de-Haute-Provence department as the road hugs the southern tip of the lake. When the road splits, take the one-way system to the right and enter the dark tunnel – beware, the road becomes two-way again immediately after exiting the tunnel. ◀

Turn left at the junction with the D900 (SP: D900/Barcelonnette) (**53km**). Follow the busy D900 through **Le Lauzet-Ubaye** (**54.5km**) and **Les Thuiles** (**68.5km**). At the roundabout on the outskirts of **Barcelonnette** take the first exit (SP: D900/Cuneo/Barcelonnette) and enter the town (**73km**). At the next roundabout take the first exit (SP: Toutes Directions) onto Quai de l'Ubaye. Follow the road to the Pont du Plan, where you will join Stage 11 of the main route (**74.6km**).

VARIANT 6

Jausiers to Saint-Sauveur-sur-Tinée

Start	Junction of the D900/Route de Restefond-Bonette, Jausiers (1219m)
Finish	Junction of the M2205/M30, Saint-Sauveur-sur-Tinée (524m)
Distance	74.75km (46½ miles)
Total ascent	1550m
Total descent	2245m
Maximum elevation	2715m
Major passes	Col de la Bonette (2715m)
Refreshments	Halte 2000 (10.8km), Bousieyas (34.1km), Le Pra (37km), Saint-Étienne-de-Tinée (46.5km), Isola (61km), Saint-Sauveur-sur-Tinée (74.7km)

Variant 6 traverses the Mercantour National Park via the striking Col de la Bonette, offering the opportunity to take a short diversion to cycle the Cime de la Bonette, a 2km circular road leading up from the pass that reaches 2802m above sea level and which lays claim to being the highest paved road in France. From the top of the Bonette a long and technical descent follows alongside the Tinée river before joining the main route just outside Saint-Sauveur-sur-Tinée.

On the northern outskirts of Jausiers take the turning off the D900 onto the Route de Restefond-Bonette (SP: Col de la Bonette Restefond/Nice). Cross the Ubaye river. Proceed on the same road, passing old military installations, all the way to the top of the wild and remote pass (**22km**).

At the top of the **Col de la Bonette**, if your legs are feeling good, you can add a further 87m in altitude to your ride by navigating the 2km loop that is the Cime de la Bonette. ▶

Opportunity for refreshments on the ascent of the Bonette is limited to the Halte 2000 Bar and Restaurant, some 12km below the pass.

The Cime de la Bonette, a 2km loop at the top of the pass, lays claim to the highest paved road in France

Route de
Haute Montagne
Absence de dispositifs
de Sécurité
Restez Vigilants

A true sign that you are about to ride a remote mountain pass

Descend from the pass following the D64/Nice, passing **Camp des Fourches** (**28.9km**) and descending through hairpins. ▶

Pass the tiny communities of **Bousieyas** (**34km**) and **Le Pra** (**37km**). The D64 swings sharply left, crossing the Pont-Haut bridge, and becomes the M2205 (**42.3km**). Enter **Saint-Étienne-de-Tinée** (**46.3km**).

The road turns sharply right and crosses a bridge. Immediately after turn left (SP: Centre Ville Parking/

The Camp des Fourches was built in 1889. One of a series of fortifications built to protect the Ubaye valley, it was the scene of fierce fighting during World War 2.

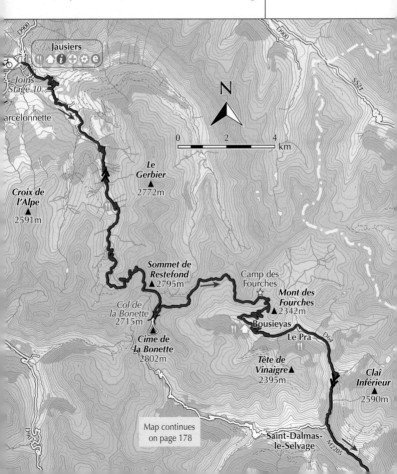

Map continues on page 178

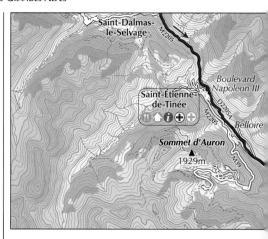

Isola-by-bike). Then turn left again (SP: Parking) now ignoring the sign for Isola by bike. Follow the narrow road, passing along Boulevard Napoléon III before emerging onto a mini-roundabout. Ignore the sign for Nice and continue straight on and pick up a cycle path to the left.

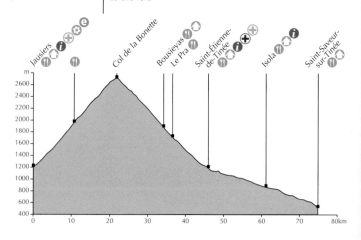

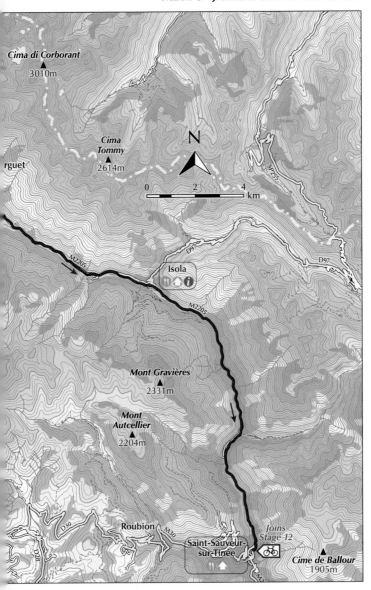

Saint-Étienne-de-Tinée provides a colourful stopping place for refreshment

The **cycle path** from Saint-Étienne-de-Tinée runs alongside the M2205A/M2205C and M2205, respectively, to Isola. At the time of the research trip the cycle path in town was closed due to storm damage. In such an event remain on the main road through Saint-Étienne-de-Tinée and pick up the path some 4km the other side of town where it joins the M2205C.

Follow the cycle path as far as **Le Bourguet** and then ignore signs for the path 50m to the right (**51.8km**). Instead, follow the M2205 road towards Isola. After passing through Cialancier rejoin the cycle path (**55.3km**) and follow into **Isola** (**60.5km**) Note: the path does rejoin the M2205 for a short time en route to Isola.

At Isola the cycle path emerges onto the M2205. Turn right and continue the long descent on the M2205. At length pass through a tunnel before reaching the junction with the M30 at **Saint-Sauveur-sur-Tinée**, where you will join Stage 12 of the main route (**74.7km**).

APPENDIX A

Bike shops and Bosch eBike charging stations

Bike shops

Stage 1
Vélo Metier
60 Av. du Général de Gaulle
74200 Thonon-les-Bains
+33 4 50 16 69 65

Culture Vélo Thonon
21 Chem. de Ronde
74200 Thonon-les-Bains
+33 4 50 26 12 87

Espace Cycles 74
43 Av. de Genève
74200 Thonon-les-Bains
+33 4 50 70 45 46

MTB Rental Morzine
95 Rte de la Combe À Zore
74110 Morzine
+33 4 50 79 02 20

L'Atelier Ski & Bike
2289 Rte des Grandes Alpes
74260 Les Gets
+33 6 80 32 86 46

Au Boitet de Yannos
24 Rte du Front de Neige
74260 Les Gets
+33 6 80 01 02 96

Véloscopie
55 Av. du Stade
74950 Scionzier
+33 4 50 90 10 20

Stage 2
Véloscopie
55 Av. du Stade
74950 Scionzier
+33 4 50 90 10 20

Oxebike
611 Rte de Thônes
Immeuble les Allobroges
74450 Saint-Jean-de-Sixt
+33 4 50 27 66 59

Stage 3
Piccard Sports
170 Av. des Jeux Olympiques
Les Saisies
73620 Hauteluce
+33 4 79 38 90 43

Stage 4
Gravitylab
297 Av. Maréchal Leclerc
73700 Bourg-Saint-Maurice
+33 4 79 40 05 54

Labo Shop
Les Jardins de Rochefort
Av. du Stade
73700 Bourg-Saint-Maurice
+33 4 79 07 07 61

Stage 5
Gravitylab
297 Av. Maréchal Leclerc
73700 Bourg-Saint-Maurice
+33 4 79 40 05 54

Labo Shop
Les Jardins de Rochefort
Av. du Stade
73700 Bourg-Saint-Maurice
+33 4 79 07 07 61

Stage 6
Intersport Rent
Rue de la Mairie
73480 Val Cenis
+33 4 79 05 89 06

Stage 7
Vélo Minute Bike Shop
Pl. de la Vanoise
73140 Saint-Michel-de-Maurienne
+33 9 72 56 31 33

Action Sports
7 Rue de la République
73500 Modane
+33 4 79 05 35 29

Magnin Sports
Rue des Grandes Alpes
73450 Valloire
+33 4 79 59 03 55

Stage 8
Magnin Sports
Rue des Grandes Alpes
73450 Valloire
+33 4 79 59 03 55

Sportrent
5 Pl. Du Vernay
05240 La Salle-les-Alpes
+33 4 92 45 16 43

Philippe Sports
Le Verney building
05240 La Salle-les-Alpes
+33 4 92 24 87 88

Mountain Cycles
Espace Sud
342 Rue du Maréchal de Lattre
de Tassigny
05100 Briançon
+33 4 92 20 52 22

Cycles And Skis
6 Av. René Froger
05100 Briançon
+33 4 92 20 40 44

Stage 9
Mountain Cycles
Espace Sud
342 Rue du Maréchal de Lattre
de Tassigny
05100 Briançon
+33 4 92 20 52 22

Cycles And Skis
6 Av. René Froger
05100 Briançon
+33 4 92 20 40 44

Loutousport
Rte du Queyras
05600 Guillestre
+33 4 92 45 24 21

Stage 10
Loutousport
Rte du Queyras
05600 Guillestre
+33 4 92 45 24 21

Jausiers Sport Technician
Grand Rue
04850 Jausiers
+33 4 92 81 13 93

Cycle Ubaye Sports
Zac du Pont Long
04400 Barcelonnette
+33 4 92 34 36 15

Stage 11
Cycle Ubaye Sports
Zac du Pont Long
04400 Barcelonnette
+33 4 92 34 36 15

Stage 12
Magasin Sport Addict
Za du Pra d'Agout
06450 Saint-Martin-Vésubie
+33 4 89 34 10 66

Stage 13
Magasin Sport Addict
Za du Pra d'Agout
06450 Saint-Martin-Vésubie
+33 4 89 34 10 66

Stage 14
Sport 21 Cycles
3 Rte de Sospel
06500 Menton
+33 4 93 86 69 51

R Bike Menton
19 Port de Garavan
06500 Menton
+33 6 26 03 31 37

Nice Bike Culture
Hibiscus Park
23 Av. Auguste Verola
06200 Nice
+33 4 93 18 59 60

Café du Cycliste
16 Quai des Docks
06300 Nice
+33 9 67 02 04 17

Variant 1
Oxebike
611 VC No Anc. Rte de Thônes À la
Clusaz
74450 Saint-Jean-de-Sixt
+33 4 50 27 66 59

Velocity Annecy
9 B Rue Louis Chaumontel
74000 Annecy
+33 7 83 80 00 90

Sassa Vélo Minute
43 Av. De France
74000 Annecy
+33 4 50 44 20 62

Culture Vélo Albertville
271 Av. Georges Pompidou
73200 Gilly-sur-Isère
+33 4 79 32 18 42

Variant 2
Gravitylab
297 Av. Maréchal Leclerc
73700 Bourg-Saint-Maurice
+33 4 79 40 05 54

Labo Shop
Les Jardins de Rochefort
Av. du Stade
73700 Bourg-Saint-Maurice
+33 4 79 07 07 61

Bike Surgery
8 Pl. Joux
73210 Aime
+33 4 57 37 69 95

Mout'n Bike
328 Av. de la Libération
73600 Moûtiers
+33 4 79 40 16 35

Sport 2000 Ravoir Sports Les 4 Vallées
Plan Mollaret
73130 Saint-François-Longchamp
+33 4 79 05 49 17

Dvélos St Jean de Maurienne
249 Rue de la Libération
73300 Saint-Jean-de-Maurienne
+33 9 87 14 98 60

Vélo Minute Bike Shop
Pl. de la Vanoise
73140 Saint-Michel-de-Maurienne
+33 9 72 56 31 33

Variant 3
Intersport Rent
Rue de la Mairie
73480 Val Cenis
+33 4 79 05 89 06

Via Norberto Rosa, 16
10059 Susa TO
Italy
+39 1 22 88 01 81

Mountain Cycles
Espace Sud 342 Rue du Maréchal de
Lattre de Tassigny
05100 Briançon
+33 4 92 20 52 22

Cycles And Skis
6 Av. René Froger
05100 Briançon
+33 4 92 20 40 44

Variant 4
Dvélos St Jean de Maurienne
249 Rue de la Libération
73300 Saint-Jean-de-Maurienne
+33 9 87 14 98 60

Vélo Minute Bike Shop
Pl. de la Vanoise
73140 Saint-Michel-de-Maurienne
+33 9 72 56 31 33

Cycles and Sports
Rue du Général de Gaulle
38520 Le Bourg-d'Oisans
+33 4 76 79 16 79

Pro Bike Support
312 Av. de la Gare
38520 Le Bourg-d'Oisans
+33 7 81 26 42 34

Variant 5
Loutousport
Rte du Queyras
05600 Guillestre
+33 4 92 45 24 21

Alpes 2 Roues
D994H
05200 Embrun
+33 4 92 43 11 10

Cycle Ubaye Sports
Zac du Pont Long
04400 Barcelonnette
+33 4 92 34 36 15

Variant 6
Jausiers Sport Technician
Grand Rue
04850 Jausiers
+33 4 92 81 13 93

Bosch eBike charge
Note: only official Bosch charging
points are shown and availability is sub-
ject to change and/or facility opening
times. Call individual facility for confir-
mation of availability. Remember, other
facilities, such as cafés and restaurants,
will often be content to let you charge a
battery while using their services.

Stage 1
Office de Tourisme
26 Pl. du Baraty
74110 Morzine
+33 4 50 74 72 72

Télésiège des Chavannes/
191–223 Route du Front de Neige
74260 Les Gets
+33 4 50 75 80 99

Sherpa Supermarché
927 Route des Grandes Alpes
74260 Les Gets
+33 4 50 79 75 18

Stage 2
None

Stage 3
Centre Aquasportif Le Signal
Les Saisies
+33 4 79 31 43 48

Stage 4
Intersport Bourg-Saint-Maurice
Zone de Super U
73700 Bourg St Maurice
+33 4 79 04 04 30

Stage 5
Intersport Bourg-Saint-Maurice
Zone de Super U
73700 Bourg St Maurice
+33 4 79 04 04 30

Office Tourisme Val d'Isère
Place Jacques Mouflier
73150 Val d'Isère
+33 4 79 06 06 60

Stage 6
Office Tourisme Val d'Isère
Place Jacques Mouflier
73150 Val d'Isère
+33 4 79 06 06 60

Sherpa Supermarché
Le Sommet de la Ville
73480 Bessans
+33 4 79 05 94 71

Hôtel Le Relais des 2 cols
66 Rue du Mont Cenis
73480 Val Cenis
+33 4 79 05 92 83

Stage 7
Maison Cantonale Modane
9 Place Sommeiller
73500 Modane
+33 4 79 05 26 67

Sherpa Supermarché Valloire
Route du Télégraphe
73450 Valloire
+33 4 79 59 96 54

Stage 8
Sherpa Supermarché Valloire
Route du Télégraphe
73450 Valloire
+33 4 79 59 96 54

Stage 9
Refuge Napoléon
Col d'Izoard
05100 Col de l'Izoard
+33 4 92 21 17 42

Stage 10
Sherpa Supermarché Vars Centre
Résidence Ski Soleil
05560 Vars
+33 4 50 79 75 18

Musée de Saint-Paul-sur-Ubaye
Le Village
04530 Saint-Paul-sur-Ubaye
+33 4 92 81 00 22

Ubaye Tourisme – Accueil de Jausiers
2–14 Grand Rue
04850 Jausiers
+33 4 92 81 21 45

Ubaye Tourisme – Accueil de
Barcelonnette
Place Frédéric Mistral
04400 Barcelonnette
+33 4 92 81 04 71

Stage 11
Ubaye Tourisme – Accueil de
Barcelonnette
Place Frédéric Mistral
04400 Barcelonnette
+33 4 92 81 04 71

Refuge – Hôtel de Bayasse
Magali Beaudoire
04400 Uvernet-Fours
+33 4 92 32 20 79

Stage 12
Vésubia Mountain Park
Allée du Dr Fulconis
06450 Saint-Martin-Vésubie
+33 4 93 23 20 30

Stage 13
Vésubia Mountain Park
Allée du Dr Fulconis
06450 Saint-Martin-Vésubie
+33 4 93 23 20 30

Stage 14
None

Variant 1
None

Variant 2
Intersport Bourg-Saint-Maurice
Zone de Super U
73700 Bourg St Maurice
+33 4 79 04 04 30

Variant 3
Hôtel Le Relais des 2 cols
66 Rue du Mont Cenis
73480 Val Cenis
+33 4 79 05 92 83

Variant 4
Hôtel Castillan
RD 1091
05320 La Grave
+33 4 76 79 90 04

Variant 5
Alpes 2 Roues
D994H
05200 Embrun
+33 4 92 43 11 10

Ubaye Tourisme – Accueil de
Barcelonnette
Place Frédéric Mistral
04400 Barcelonnette
+33 4 92 81 04 71

Variant 6
Ubaye Tourisme – Accueil de Jausiers
2–14 Grand Rue
04850 Jausiers
+33 4 92 81 21 45

APPENDIX B
Recommended cycling essentials checklist

Bike equipment/spares
Good-quality front and rear lights
Spare inner tubes
Puncture repair kit
Foldable spare tyre
Pump
Tyre levers
Multi-tool/Allen keys
Chain tool
Chain link connectors
Spoke key
Adjustable spanner
Brake blocks (if rim brakes)
Disc brake pads (if disc brakes)
Battery charger (if eBike)
Cable ties
Spare bolts
Bike lock

Cycling clothing/luggage
Helmet
Hi-vis cycling jersey
Good-quality base layer
Cycling shorts/knicks
Cycling gloves
Cycling socks
Cycling shoes
Neck warmer/snood
Gilet
Hi-vis waterproof jacket
Waterproof cap
Waterproof cycling leggings/trousers
Waterproof overshoes
Arm and leg warmers
Tinted/clear-lensed glasses
Small waist bag
Waterproof dry bag
Panniers

Extras
Water bottle/bidon
First-aid kit
Sunscreen
Environmentally friendly wet wipes
Map
Phone and charger
Guidebook
Pen
Money, credit/debit cards
UK to Europe electric plug adaptor

APPENDIX C
Useful resources and essential information

Below is a list of websites and resources that may prove helpful both prior to and during a trip to the RdGA. Please note that many of the listed resources will also have mobile applications available for download.

General

www.routedesgrandesalpes.com
RdGA website

www.parcsnationaux.fr
France national parks website

www.meteofrance.com
France national meteorological

www.yr.no
Detailed mountain weather forecasts

www.cols-cyclisme.com
Information re status of mountain passes

www.inforoute05.fr
Road/mountain pass info for Haute-Alpes dept

www.inforoute74.fr
Road/mountain pass info for Haute-Savoie dept

www.savoie-route.fr
Road/mountain pass info for Savoie dept

www.inforoute04.fr
Road/mountain pass info for Alpes-de-Haute-Provence dept

www.inforoutes06.fr
Road/mountain pass info for Alpes-Maritime dept

translate.google.co.uk
Translation service

www.bing.com/translator
Translation service

www.microsoft.com/en-us/translator/
Translation service app

www.cyclinguk.org
General cycling information

www.gov.uk
Current travel advice

Transportation

www.eurostar.com
Rail travel from London to France

www.sncf.com/en
France rail operator

www.trainline.com
European rail tickets

www.raileurope.com
European rail tickets

seat61.com
Rail information

www.flixbus.co.uk
International coach travel

www.blablacar.co.uk
International coach travel/car share

www.transalis.fr
Geneva and wider area bus company

www.shuttledirect.com
Private transfers around Geneva area

www.alpinecab.co.uk
Private transfers around Geneva area

www.bcyclet.com
Bicycle hire company with delivery and collection service

www.sanef.com
France motorway operator

www.eurotunnel.com
Channel Tunnel bookings

www.dfds.com
DFDS Ferries

www.poferries.com
P&O Ferries

www.directferries.co.uk
Ferry comparison website

www.gva.ch/en
Geneva airport website

www.nice.aeroport.fr
Nice airport website

www.skyscanner.net
Flight comparison website

Accommodation

www.booking.com
Catered and S/C accommodation finder

www.airbnb.com
Catered and S/C accommodation finder

www.chambres-hotes.fr
Gites and B&B finder

www.campingfrance.com
Campsite finder

www.hihostels.com
Hostel finder

Organised and supported tours

www.velorizons.com
www.larebenne.com
www.bike-alive.com

Tourist offices A–Z

Town	Stage(s)	Address/phone/website
Aime	V2	1139 Av. de la Tarentaise, 73210 Aime +33 4 79 55 67 00 www.la-plagne.com
Albertville	V1	15 Av. de Winnenden, 73200 Albertville +33 4 79 32 04 22 www.pays-albertville.com
Allemont	V4	400 Rte des Fonderies Royales, 38114 Allemont +33 4 76 80 71 60 www.oisans.com
Annecy	V1	Lac d, 1 Rue Jean Jaurès, 74000 Annecy +33 4 50 45 00 33 www.lac-annecy.com
Barcelonnette	S10/11, V5	Place Frédéric Mistral, 04400 Barcelonnette +33 4 92 81 04 71 www.barcelonnette.com
Beaufort	S3/4	2 Grande Rue, 73270 Beaufort +33 4 79 38 37 57 www.areches-beaufort.com
Bonneval-sur-Arc	S6	Résidence Ciamarella, 73480 Bonneval-sur-Arc +33 4 79 05 95 95 www.bonneval-sur-arc.com
Bourg-d'Oisans	V4	Quai Dr Girard, 38520 Le Bourg-d'Oisans +33 4 76 80 03 25 www.bourgdoisans.com
Bourg-Saint- Maurice	S4/5, V2	Pl. de la Gare, 73700 Bourg-Saint-Maurice + 33 4 79 07 12 57 www.lesarcs.com
Briançon	S8/9, V3	Rue Centrale, 05100 Briançon +33 4 92 24 98 98 www.serre-chevalier.com
Cesana Torinese	V3	Piazza Vittorio Amedeo, 3, 10054 Cesana Torinese TO, Italy +39 01 22 89 202 www.turismotorino.org

Town	Stage(s)	Address/phone/website
Cluses	S1/2	100 Pl. du 11 Novembre, 74300 Cluses +33 4 50 96 69 69 www.cluses-montagnes-tourisme.com
Embrun	V5	Pl. Gén Dosse, 05200 Embrun +33 4 92 43 72 72 www.serreponcon-tourisme.com
Guillaumes	S12	Pl. de Provence, 06470 Guillaumes +33 4 93 05 57 76 www.guillaumes.fr
Guillestre	S9/10, V5	Pl. Joseph Salva, 05600 Guillestre +33 4 92 24 77 61 www.guillestroisqueyras.com
Isola	V6	Pl. Jean Gaissa, 06420 Isola +33 4 93 23 23 00
Jausiers	S10, V6	12–14 Grand Rue, 04850 Jausiers +33 4 92 81 21 45 www.jausiers.com
La Chambre	V2	Résidence Les Charmettes, 73130 La Chambre +33 4 79 56 33 58 www.tourisme-la-chambre.com
La Clusaz	S2/3	161 Pl. de l'Église, 74220 La Clusaz +33 4 50 32 65 00 www.laclusaz.com
La Grave	V4	RD 1091, 05320 La Grave +33 4 76 79 90 05 www.lagrave-lameije.com
La-Salle-les-Alpes	S8	Centre Commercial, Rte de Pré-Long, 05240 La Salle-les-Alpes +33 4 92 24 98 98 www.serre-chevalier.com
Le Grand-Bornand	S2	62 Pl. de l'Église, 74450 Le Grand-Bornand +33 4 50 02 78 00 www.legrandbornand.com
Le Reposoir	S2	85 Chemin de Fréchet, 74950 Le Reposoir +33 4 50 98 18 01 www.lereposoir.fr
Les Gets	S1	89 Rte du Front de Neige, 74260 Les Gets +33 4 50 74 74 74 www.lesgets.com
Les Saisies	S3	316 Av. des Jeux Olympiques, 73620 Hauteluce +33 4 79 38 90 30 www.lessaisies.com
Lescheraines	V1	Av. Denis Therme, 73630 Le Châtelard +33 4 79 54 84 28 www.lesbauges.com
Le Monêtier-les-Bains	S8	Rte de Grenoble, 05220 Le Monêtier-les-Bains +33 4 92 24 98 98 www.serre-chevalier.com
Menton	S14	8 Av. Boyer, 06500 Menton +33 4 83 93 70 20 www.menton-riviera-merveilles.fr
Modane	7	9 Pl. Sommeiller, 73500 Modane +33 4 79 05 10 54 www.cchautemaurienne.com
Montgenèvre	V3	Place du Bivouac Napoléon – Route d'Italie, 05100 Montgenèvre +33 4 92 21 52 52 www.montgenevre.com

Town	Stage(s)	Address/phone/website
Morzine	S1	26 Pl. du Baraty, 74110 Morzine +33 4 50 74 72 72 www.morzine-avoriaz.com
Moûtiers	V2	80 Sq. de la Liberté, 73600 Moûtiers +33 4 79 04 29 05 www.coeurdetarentaise-tourisme.com
Nice	S14	5 Prom. des Anglais, 06000 Nice +33 4 92 14 46 14 www.nicetourisme.com
Oulx	V3	Piazza Aldo Garambois, 2, 10056 Oulx TO, Italy +39 01 22 83 23 69 www.turismo-oulx.it
Roquebillière	S13	26 Pl. du Général Corniglion Molinier, 06450 Roquebillière +33 4 93 03 51 60 www.nicetourisme.com
Saint-Étienne-de-Tinée	V6	Place de l'Église, 06660 Saint-Étienne-de-Tinée +33 4 93 02 41 96 www.auron.com
Saint-François-Longchamp	V2	Maison du Tourisme, 73130 Saint-François-Longchamp +33 4 79 59 10 56 www.saintfrancoislongchamp.com
Saint-Jean-d'Arves	V4	D80B, 73530 Saint-Jean-d'Arves +33 4 79 59 73 30 www.sja73.com
Saint-Jean-de-Maurienne	V2	Ancien Evêché, Pl. de la Cathédrale, 73300 Saint-Jean-de-Maurienne +33 4 79 83 51 51 www.montagnicimes.com
Saint-Jean-de-Sixt	S1, V1	47chemin Léon Laydernier, 74450 Saint-Jean-de-Sixt +33 4 50 02 70 14 www.saintjeandesixt.com
Saint-Martin-Vésubie	S12/13	Pl. du Général de Gaulle, 06450 Saint-Martin-Vésubie +33 4 93 03 21 28 www.saintmartinvesubie.fr
Saint-Michel-de-Maurienne	S7, V4	36 Rue Général Ferrié, 73140 Saint-Michel-de-Maurienne +33 4 79 56 52 54 www.maurienne-galibier.com
Saint-Étienne-de-Tinée	V6	Place de l'Église, 06660 Saint-Étienne-de-Tinée +33 4 93 02 41 96 www.auron.com
Savines-le-Lac	V5	9 Av. de la Combe d'Or, 05160 Savines-le-Lac +33 4 92 44 31 00 www.serreponcon-tourisme.com
Sospel	S13/14	1 Pl. Saint-Pierre, 06380 Sospel +33 4 83 93 95 70 www.menton-riviera-merveilles.fr
St-Pierre-d'Albigny	V1	Rue Auguste Domenget, 73250 Saint-Pierre-d'Albigny +33 4 79 25 53 12 www.tourisme.coeurdesavoie.fr
Susa	V3	Corso Inghilterra, 39, 10059 Susa TO, Italy +39 0122 622447 www.turismotorino.org
Thônes	V1	1 Rue Blanche, 74230 Thônes +33 4 50 02 00 26 www.thonescoeurdesvallees.com

Town	Stage(s)	Address/phone/website
Thonon-les-Bains	S1	2 Rue Michaud, 74200 Thonon-les-Bains +33 4 50 71 55 55 www.thononlesbains.com
Val d'Isère	S5/6	Place Jacques Mouflier, 73150 Val d'Isère +33 4 79 06 06 60 www.valdisere.com
Valberg	S11/12	Pl. Charles Ginesy, 06470 Péone +33 4 93 23 24 25 www.valberg.com
Val Cenis Lanslebourg	S6	89 Rue du Mont Cenis, 73480 Val Cenis +33 4 79 05 99 06 www.haute-maurienne-vanoise.com
Val Cenis Lanslevillard	S6, V3	Rue sous l'Église, 73480 Val Cenis +33 4 79 05 99 15 www.haute-maurienne-vanoise.com
Val Cenis Termignon	S6/7	Pl. de la Vanoise, 73500 Val Cenis +33 4 79 20 51 67 www.haute-maurienne-vanoise.com
Valloire	S7/8	Rue des Grandes Alpes, 73450 Valloire +33 4 79 59 03 96 www.valloire.net
Vars	S10	Cr Fontanarosa, 05560 Vars +33 4 92 46 51 31 www.vars.com

France essential information:

Emergency telephone number: 112

International dialling code: +33

Currency: Euro

Typical banking hours: 0900–1200 and 1400–1700 Monday to Friday

Typical pharmacy hours: 0930–1200 and 1400–1900 Monday to Saturday

Credit/debit cards: Visa and Mastercard widely accepted in urban areas

Electricity: 230V-50Hz;
2-pin plug types C and E

UK nationals' entry requirements: Passport valid for at least three months after the planned day of departure from France. Visa-free travel for stays of 90 days or fewer over a 180-day period.

Emergency healthcare: State-provided medical treatment for EHIC/GHIC holders on same basis as French nationals.

Covid restrictions: Check www.gov.uk/foreign-travel-advice/france/coronavirus for current situation.

Identity documents: to be produced upon request by police or within four hours at a police station. Accepted documents include passport or photo driving licence.

Check www.gov.uk/foreign-travel-advice/france for all latest UK Government advice and information on travel in France.

APPENDIX D
Glossary of cycling specific terms

English	French
battery	*batterie*
bell	*sonnette*
bicycle lane	*voie cyclable*
bicycle pump	*pompe vélo*
bicycle rack	*range-vélos*
bottle cage	*porte-bidon*
brakes (front/rear)	*freins (avant/arrière)*
cable	*câble*
cassette	*cassette*
chain	*chaîne (de vélo)*
chainwheel	*plateau*
derailleur (front/rear)	*dérailleur (avant/arrière)*
fork	*fourche*
frame	*cadre*
handlebars	*guidon*
helmet	*casque de vélo*

English	French
lights	*eclairage*
luggage carrier	*porte-bagages*
motor	*moteur*
mudguard	*garde-boue*
pedal	*pédale*
reflectors	*réflecteurs (m)*
rim	*jante*
saddle	*selle*
saddlebag	*sacoche de selle*
shock-absorber	*amortisseur*
spindle	*axe*
spoke	*rayon*
toe clip	*cale-pied*
tyre	*pneu*
valve	*valve*
wheel	*roue*

NOTES

NOTES

Looking down on Plan Lachat as the Galibier really kicks in (Stage 8)

DOWNLOAD THE ROUTES
IN GPX FORMAT

All the routes in this guide are available for download from:

www.cicerone.co.uk/1054/GPX

as standard format GPX files. You should be able to load them into most online GPX systems and mobile devices, whether GPS or smartphone. You may need to convert the file into your preferred format using a conversion programme such as gpsvisualizer.com or one of the many other such websites and programmes.

When you follow this link, you will be asked for your email address and where you purchased the guidebook, and have the option to subscribe to the Cicerone e-newsletter.

www.cicerone.co.uk

LISTING OF CICERONE GUIDES

BRITISH ISLES CHALLENGES, COLLECTIONS AND ACTIVITIES

Cycling Land's End to John o' Groats
The Big Rounds
The Book of the Bivvy
The Book of the Bothy
The Mountains of England & Wales:
    Vol 1 Wales
    Vol 2 England
The National Trails
Walking The End to End Trail

SCOTLAND

Ben Nevis and Glen Coe
Cycle Touring in Northern Scotland
Cycling in the Hebrides
Great Mountain Days in Scotland
Mountain Biking in Southern and
    Central Scotland
Mountain Biking in West and North
    West Scotland
Not the West Highland Way
Scotland
Scotland's Best Small Mountains
Scotland's Mountain Ridges
Skye's Cuillin Ridge Traverse
The Borders Abbeys Way
The Great Glen Way
The Great Glen Way Map Booklet
The Hebridean Way
The Hebrides
The Isle of Mull
The Isle of Skye
The Skye Trail
The Southern Upland Way
The Speyside Way
The Speyside Way Map Booklet
The West Highland Way
The West Highland Way
    Map Booklet
Walking Ben Lawers, Rannoch
    and Atholl
Walking in the Cairngorms
Walking in the Pentland Hills
Walking in the Scottish Borders
Walking in the Southern Uplands
Walking in Torridon
Walking Loch Lomond and
    the Trossachs
Walking on Arran
Walking on Harris and Lewis
Walking on Jura, Islay and Colonsay
Walking on Rum and the Small Isles
Walking on the Orkney and
    Shetland Isles
Walking on Uist and Barra
Walking the Cape Wrath Trail
Walking the Corbetts
    Vol 1 South of the Great Glen
    Vol 2 North of the Great Glen

Walking the Galloway Hills
Walking the Munros
    Vol 1 – Southern, Central and
        Western Highlands
    Vol 2 – Northern Highlands and
        the Cairngorms
Winter Climbs Ben Nevis and
    Glen Coe
Winter Climbs in the Cairngorms

NORTHERN ENGLAND ROUTES

Cycling the Reivers Route
Cycling the Way of the Roses
Hadrian's Cycleway
Hadrian's Wall Path
Hadrian's Wall Path Map Booklet
The C2C Cycle Route
The Coast to Coast Walk
The Coast to Coast Map Booklet
The Pennine Way
The Pennine Way Map Booklet
Walking the Dales Way
Walking the Dales Way Map Booklet

NORTH EAST ENGLAND, YORKSHIRE DALES AND PENNINES

Cycling in the Yorkshire Dales
Great Mountain Days in
    the Pennines
Mountain Biking in the
    Yorkshire Dales
St Oswald's Way and
    St Cuthbert's Way
The Cleveland Way and the
    Yorkshire Wolds Way
The Cleveland Way Map Booklet
The North York Moors
The Reivers Way
The Teesdale Way
Trail and Fell Running in the
    Yorkshire Dales
Walking in County Durham
Walking in Northumberland
Walking in the North Pennines
Walking in the Yorkshire Dales:
    North and East
Walking in the Yorkshire Dales:
    South and West

NORTH WEST ENGLAND AND THE ISLE OF MAN

Cycling the Pennine Bridleway
Isle of Man Coastal Path
The Lancashire Cycleway
The Lune Valley and Howgills
Walking in Cumbria's Eden Valley
Walking in Lancashire
Walking in the Forest of Bowland
    and Pendle
Walking on the Isle of Man

Walking on the West Pennine Moors
Walks in Silverdale and Arnside

LAKE DISTRICT

Cycling in the Lake District
Great Mountain Days in the
    Lake District
Joss Naylor's Lakes, Meres and
    Waters of the Lake District
Lake District Winter Climbs
Lake District: High Level and
    Fell Walks
Lake District: Low Level and
    Lake Walks
Mountain Biking in the Lake District
Outdoor Adventures with Children –
    Lake District
Scrambles in the Lake District –
    North
Scrambles in the Lake District –
    South
The Cumbria Way
Trail and Fell Running in the
    Lake District
Walking the Lake District Fells –
    Borrowdale
    Buttermere
    Coniston
    Keswick
    Langdale
    Mardale and the Far East
    Patterdale
    Wasdale
Walking the Tour of the Lake District

DERBYSHIRE, PEAK DISTRICT AND MIDLANDS

Cycling in the Peak District
Dark Peak Walks
Scrambles in the Dark Peak
Walking in Derbyshire
Walking in the Peak District –
    White Peak East
Walking in the Peak District –
    White Peak West

SOUTHERN ENGLAND

20 Classic Sportive Rides in
    South East England
20 Classic Sportive Rides in
    South West England
Cycling in the Cotswolds
Mountain Biking on the
    North Downs
Mountain Biking on the
    South Downs
North Downs Way Map Booklet
Walking the South West Coast Path
South West Coast Path Map Booklets
    Vol 1: Minehead to St Ives
    Vol 2: St Ives to Plymouth
    Vol 3: Plymouth to Poole

Shorter Walks in the Dolomites
Ski Touring and Snowshoeing in the Dolomites
The Way of St Francis
Trekking in the Apennines
Trekking in the Dolomites
Trekking the Giants' Trail: Alta Via 1 through the Italian Pennine Alps
Via Ferratas of the Italian Dolomites Vols 1&2
Walking and Trekking in the Gran Paradiso
Walking in Abruzzo
Walking in Italy's Cinque Terre
Walking in Italy's Stelvio National Park
Walking in Sicily
Walking in the Dolomites
Walking in Tuscany
Walking in Umbria
Walking Lake Como and Maggiore
Walking Lake Garda and Iseo
Walking on the Amalfi Coast
Walking the Via Francigena pilgrim route – Parts 2&3
Walks and Treks in the Maritime Alps

MEDITERRANEAN

The High Mountains of Crete
Trekking in Greece
Treks and Climbs in Wadi Rum, Jordan
Walking and Trekking in Zagori
Walking and Trekking on Corfu
Walking in Cyprus
Walking on Malta
Walking on the Greek Islands – the Cyclades

NEW ZEALAND & AUSTRALIA

Hiking the Overland Track

NORTH AMERICA

The John Muir Trail
The Pacific Crest Trail

SOUTH AMERICA

Aconcagua and the Southern Andes
Hiking and Biking Peru's Inca Trails
Torres del Paine

SCANDINAVIA, ICELAND AND GREENLAND

Hiking in Norway – South
Trekking in Greenland – The Arctic Circle Trail
Trekking the Kungsleden
Walking and Trekking in Iceland

SLOVENIA, CROATIA, MONTENEGRO AND ALBANIA

Mountain Biking in Slovenia
The Islands of Croatia
The Julian Alps of Slovenia
The Mountains of Montenegro
The Peaks of the Balkans Trail
The Slovene Mountain Trail
Walking in Slovenia: The Karavanke
Walks and Treks in Croatia

SPAIN AND PORTUGAL

Camino de Santiago: Camino Frances
Coastal Walks in Andalucia
Cycling the Camino de Santiago
Cycling the Ruta Via de la Plata
Mountain Walking in Mallorca
Mountain Walking in Southern Catalunya
Portugal's Rota Vicentina
Spain's Sendero Historico: The GR1
The Andalucian Coast to Coast Walk
The Camino del Norte and Camino Primitivo
The Camino Ingles and Ruta do Mar
The Camino Portugues
The Mountains of Nerja
The Mountains of Ronda and Grazalema
The Sierras of Extremadura
Trekking in Mallorca
Trekking in the Canary Islands
Trekking the GR7 in Andalucia
Walking and Trekking in the Sierra Nevada
Walking in Andalucia
Walking in Menorca
Walking in Portugal
Walking in the Algarve
Walking in the Cordillera Cantabrica
Walking on Gran Canaria
Walking on La Gomera and El Hierro
Walking on La Palma
Walking on Lanzarote and Fuerteventura
Walking on Madeira
Walking on Tenerife
Walking on the Azores
Walking on the Costa Blanca
Walking the Camino dos Faros

SWITZERLAND

Switzerland's Jura Crest Trail
The Swiss Alpine Pass Route – Via Alpina Route 1
The Swiss Alps
Tour of the Jungfrau Region
Walking in the Bernese Oberland
Walking in the Engadine – Switzerland
Walking in the Valais
Walking in Zermatt and Saas-Fee

JAPAN AND ASIA

Hiking and Trekking in the Japan Alps and Mount Fuji
Japan's Kumano Kodo Pilgrimage
Trekking in Tajikistan

HIMALAYA

Annapurna
Everest: A Trekker's Guide
Trekking in Bhutan
Trekking in Ladakh
Trekking in the Himalaya

MOUNTAIN LITERATURE

8000 metres
A Walk in the Clouds
Abode of the Gods
Fifty Years of Adventure
The Pennine Way – the Path, the People, the Journey
Unjustifiable Risk?

TECHNIQUES

Fastpacking
Geocaching in the UK
Map and Compass
Outdoor Photography
Polar Exploration
The Mountain Hut Book

MINI GUIDES

Alpine Flowers
Navigation
Pocket First Aid and Wilderness Medicine
Snow

CICERONE

Trust Cicerone to guide your next adventure, wherever it may be around the world...

Discover guides for hiking, mountain walking, backpacking, trekking, trail running, cycling and mountain biking, ski touring, climbing and scrambling in Britain, Europe and worldwide.

Connect with Cicerone online and find inspiration.

- buy books and ebooks
- articles, advice and trip reports
- podcasts and live events
- GPX files and updates
- regular newsletter

cicerone.co.uk